TRAINING YOUR DOG
FOR SPORTS AND
OTHER ACTIVITIES

Charlotte Schwartz

TS-258

Dedication

This book is dedicated to Ginger, my little apricot Poodle who shares life with me. Not only is she a wonderful companion, but she's bright and willing to please, has a terrific sense of humor, and is always willing to try some new idea that pops into my head for doing things together.

Title page: Golden Retriever clearing the bar jump at an agility trial. Photo by Karen Taylor.

© 1996 by T.F.H. Publications, Inc.

Distributed in the UNITED STATES to the Pet Trade by T.F.H. Publications, Inc., One T.F.H. Plaza, Neptune City, NJ 07753; distributed in the UNITED STATES to the Bookstore and Library Trade by National Book Network, Inc. 4720 Boston Way, Lanham MD 20706; in CANADA to the Pet Trade by H & L Pet Supplies Inc., 27 Kingston Crescent, Kitchener, Ontario N2B 2T6; Rolf C. Hagen Ltd., 3225 Sartelon Street, Montreal 382 Quebec; in CANADA to the Book Trade by Vanwell Publishing Ltd., 1 Northrup Crescent, St. Catharines, Ontario L2M 6P5 ; in ENGLAND by T.F.H. Publications, PO Box 15, Waterlooville PO7 6BQ; in AUSTRALIA AND THE SOUTH PACIFIC by T.F.H. (Australia), Pty. Ltd., Box 149, Brookvale 2100 N.S.W., Australia; in NEW ZEALAND by Brooklands Aquarium Ltd. 5 McGiven Drive, New Plymouth, RD1 New Zealand; in Japan by T.F.H. Publications, Japan—Jiro Tsuda, 10-12-3 Ohjidai, Sakura, Chiba 285, Japan; in SOUTH AFRICA by Lopis (Pty) Ltd., P.O. Box 39127, Booysens, 2016, Johannesburg, South Africa. Published by T.F.H. Publications, Inc.
MANUFACTURED IN THE UNITED STATES OF AMERICA
BY T.F.H. PUBLICATIONS, INC.

Contents

Preface

Somewhere along the way to civilization, mankind and canines formed an allegiance to live and work together for the betterment of both species. When the union finally solidified and people began bringing dogs into the home, however, it was not without problems.

The humans had to learn to live and communicate with their new cohabitants. The dogs had to learn to cope with the idiosyncrasies of their two-legged friends. Both had to readjust their social structure to include each other and benefit from this new arrangement.

Man, being the more sophisticated and vocal of the two, assumed leadership. With that step, dog training became a fact of life. For some, training the family pet was approached on a formal basis. For others, it happened out of necessity and was often a hit-or-miss proposition.

Whatever the method or the level of expertise of the teacher, the student tried to comprehend and adapt his ways to that of his bipedal partner. Oh, there's always been the cantankerous individual who resisted change and learning, but if the general population of canines hadn't been willing to adapt, the species would never have survived.

At any rate, the more man and dog succeeded in developing a working relationship with each other, the broader their horizons became. Today, as for the past several thousand years, dogs are an integral part of

The author and her apricot Poodle, Ginger, enjoy a leisurely bicycle ride.

Zach and a six-week-old Shar-Pei puppy bred by Melvard's Trendsetter Shar-Pei cool off by the pool on a hot summer day. Photo by Isabelle Francais.

and people who were living together yet whose relationship left a lot to be desired. The dogs liked the people, the people liked the dogs, but it was obvious that the strong bond necessary for a full and satisfying relationship was missing.

We know dogs are social animals, but we frequently forget that living with a pack is not enough for man or dog. Each individual must have a place in the pack and do his or her share to keep the pack functioning. Providing he understands his place in the social structure and contributes to the survival of that structure, he's a happy, well-adjusted

Above: Riverwind The Little Mermaid, a red longhaired Dachshund owned by Judy Thompson, gives an affectionate lick to her human friend. Photo by Isabelle Francais. *Right:* A well-dressed young man and a Brittany, owned by Karen Wagner, pose for a picture before a conformation show. Photo by Isabelle Francais.

mankind's life, both at work and play.

It has often occurred to me that no one has ever written a book for pet owners telling all about these activities, giving instructions and listing additional contacts. Oh, there are books detailing specific behaviors, some with full instructions. But I've never been able to find one book giving the pet owner a wide variety of ideas to help him make his dog a more integral part of the family.

Being a dog obedience instructor for over 25 years has given me ample opportunity to witness dogs

Dogs make great play-mates for children. Dalmatian owned by Ben Riley. Photo by Isabelle Francais.

individual. But without a purpose and a strong bond with his pack, his behavior often becomes neurotic because his life is useless and meaningless.

Then, one day, out of sheer frustration with a particular client and his unruly, yet pleasant dog, I identified the missing element—a purpose. The dog and man lacked a purpose for their relationship. Their love for each other simply floated aimlessly like a little lamb running around the pasture looking for its mother.

Once we customized a training program for them, the man felt a lot better about his dog because the dog learned to learn and exhibited a willingness to work with his owner. In other words, they developed a bond between them. This bond, together with a specific job that the dog was trained to perform

Dogs can teach children a lot about responsibility and commitment. *Right:* Merimaurs Cases Show Time, a nine-month-old Pomeranian owned by Susan Lucatorto. Photo by Isabelle Francais. *Below:* Barstar's Chocolate Chips MS, a miniature Dachshund owned by Barbara Starnes. Photo by Isabelle Francais.

for his owner, created the ideal atmosphere for a rewarding relationship for both man and the dog.

The dog's unruliness disappeared and the man later commented that he considered the whole episode just a bad dream. But, as his instructor, I knew how hard he had worked at reversing the dog's undesirable behavior to produce instead a fine partner who gave him great pride of ownership.

I have repeated this little vignette a thousand times over the years. In fact, I've developed a whole collage

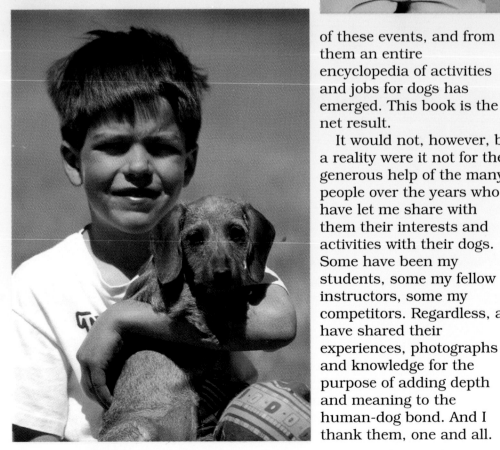

of these events, and from them an entire encyclopedia of activities and jobs for dogs has emerged. This book is the net result.

It would not, however, be a reality were it not for the generous help of the many people over the years who have let me share with them their interests and activities with their dogs. Some have been my students, some my fellow instructors, some my competitors. Regardless, all have shared their experiences, photographs and knowledge for the purpose of adding depth and meaning to the human-dog bond. And I thank them, one and all.

A puppy's love is unconditional. This Rottweiler puppy is owned by Juan and Nancy Griego. Photo by Isabelle Francais.

Keeping in mind the various types of dogs in the world—big, little, active, passive, dominant, submissive, etc.—and an equally interesting variety of people—old, young, athletic, introverted, extroverted, etc.—I've tried to include something for everyone. There are behaviors to teach city dogs, country dogs, farm dogs, traveling dogs, etc. And finally, there are activities for dogs and people who never leave a tiny apartment as well as those who make the whole world their home.

As long as there are dogs and owners and people who work with them such as trainers, instructors, behaviorists and health care professionals, those dogs and owners will be learning more and more about how to live life to the fullest together. It is my desire to have this book become a valuable part of that process.

Your Canine Companion

NATURAL INSTINCTS

When deciding what type of activity you'd like to get your dog involved in, one must first take into consideration the dog's natural instincts for performing the activity. For example, a dog that's been bred to hunt by using his nose would be a natural for scenting activities. A natural retriever would probably take to fetching like a duck to water, and a dog whose ancestors have been pulling sleds over the Arctic ice for centuries would love pulling a wagon.

This is not to say that a dog can learn only what it's been bred to do; it can learn as much as you, the owner, desire to teach it.

But starting out by teaching an activity that comes naturally to the dog will assure you both of a high rate of success. Once that behavior is mastered, you and your dog will have a better line of communication and understanding so that learning more difficult activities later on is much easier.

With this in mind, it would be prudent to investigate the history and purpose for which your dog (providing he or she is a purebred) was originally developed. In the case of a mixed breed, having some idea of what breeds went into its makeup will help. But, studying the dog to determine what it does naturally and seems to enjoy doing will help you plan not only what you're going to teach it but how you'll approach the training as well.

PHYSICAL ABILITY

Common sense tells us that we would never consider teaching a Toy Poodle to retrieve a telephone receiver that is hanging on a wall or a Great Dane to fetch your slippers from under the bed when his

Herding breeds, such as the Australian Shepherd, are agile and intelligent. Here, Cassie moves a herd of sheep in Montana. Photo by Judith Strom.

The instincts of gundogs remain strong even today. This Labrador Retriever and his master are returning from a successful hunting trip. Owners, Kathy and Ted McCue. Photo by Isabelle Francais.

Some activities require more agility than others. As a breed, Dalmatians are athletic and energetic. Photo by Karen Taylor.

head won't fit under the bed. The size of your dog is an important consideration. Never attempt to teach a dog something that he is physically incapable of doing. In other words, fit the activity to the dog and you'll both succeed.

There are several other things we need to think about before making a final decision regarding dog activities. Taking the time to think through these things now may save a lot of trouble, wasted time and heartache later on.

The dog's sex, age, weight, and condition are equally important. Ask yourself questions that will help you analyze how well

suited your dog is to a particular activity.

Is the dog overweight? Underweight? In good health and/or physical condition? After all, you'd hardly expect a fat, elderly dog to go jogging 14 miles a day with you when he hasn't had more than a daily ten-minute walk all his life. Some activities require much more agility than others, too. Can your dog handle it?

Conversely, it would be unrealistic to expect a rambunctious puppy to learn an activity that requires patience and a prolonged period of total concentration. Let the puppy be a puppy and enjoy his growing-up months. When he's mature, he'll be more than willing and able to learn such complicated activities as scent hurdle racing and signal exercises.

Teach puppies and young dogs activities that they are mentally, emotionally, and physically capable of learning; leave the difficult activities to the healthy, mature dog.

Sex is another important factor. The behavior of intact dogs, both males and females, can be, and often is, highly influenced by their hormones. Generally, spayed females and neutered males are much more tractable and eager to please simply because their behavior is not controlled by hormones as in the case of intact individuals. Furthermore, the dogs themselves have no idea why they behave the way they do and are usually powerless to change it without surgical intervention.

Some activities will demand more self-control from the dog than others. If, for example, you have a strong-willed, intact male who doesn't get along well with other males, you wouldn't choose an activity such as lure coursing or scent hurdle racing, which requires him to participate independently with other males. And, of course, if you intend to train an intact female to perform certain activities and she comes into season twice a year, that may hamper her ability to function beyond

The Golden Retriever is a strong swimmer, making water sports ideal activities for owners of this breed. Photo by Isabelle Francais.

Brittany and his owner getting their exercise on a jogging path. Photo by Judith Strom.

the tight security of her home during those times.

You can see, then, that considering all of the aspects of your own dog and matching them to the specifics of any activity is the first step in integrating your dog into your lifestyle and interests. A few minutes of careful planning now will go a long way in assuring you success in the future.

YOUR INVOLVEMENT WITH YOUR DOG

Now, let's turn our attention to you, the owner, before we make that final decision for your dog. How much time do you have to spend in teaching and practicing the activity with your dog? Some activities take infinitely more time

and patience than others. To be successful, you need to familiarize yourself with exactly what's involved with each activity under consideration before you make up your mind.

Some activities, as pointed out earlier, are naturals for your dog. These are ideal activities for the busy dog owner who has little time to spend in formal training to teach his dog. And some of the activities listed are simply extensions of things you probably already do now by yourself. Swimming, walking, boating, and camping are such activities that would take very little effort from you to involve the dog. And, if he's like most dogs, he'll enjoy participating in your activities.

Highlands Sprite, CDX, UCD, CGC, a Border Collie, playing with owner Joan Fleming. Photo by Isabelle Francais.

When you think you've hit on just the right activity, ask yourself how motivated you really are to teach this particular activity to your dog. Have you thought objectively about your dog's potential? It isn't fair to expect more of him than he's capable of giving you. The capability to learn a specific activity, enjoy it and, in the process, give you a feeling of reward and fulfillment are within every dog's potential. It remains for you, the owner, to decide exactly what that activity will be.

If the activity you wish to teach your dog is to be functional as well as fun for him, you should choose one that will utilize the dog's help to benefit you and allow him to perform the task frequently enough for it to be rewarding for him. Teaching a dog to pull a snow sled would be an exercise in futility if you live in Florida. And training a dog to carry a newspaper in from the front yard would be useless if you don't get a newspaper delivered regularly. A dog needs to perform his activity frequently, say twice weekly at the least, preferably daily. So choose a job that will help make your life a little easier and allow the dog to perform it as often as possible.

When you think about it, herding dogs work all day every day with their

This young lady is teaching an English Springer Spaniel puppy to walk on a leash. Owner Kathy Kirk. Photo by Isabelle Francais.

As companions, toy dogs cannot be beat. This Miniature Pinscher is owned by Tina M. Monninger.

in organized field trials, racing requires a team for competition, obedience trials must have more than one entry, and Schutzhund work can only be accomplished with assistance from other people.

Training a dog to perform a specific activity and then finding that you and your dog are alone and miles away from the nearest other dog/owner team can be very disappointing. In this book, full particulars are given under the section of each activity as to whether or not group support is necessary. And if so, names and addresses are given so you can obtain help and information regarding that activity.

However, there are many activities listed that require no one other than yourself in order for the dog to learn and function. In a few, a person can find as much fun teaching his dog an activity at home as he can in becoming involved in that same activity along with a group. In fact, there are activities in this book that are designed to provide something for everyone: people and dogs that love the social aspect of an activity, people and dogs who are geographically isolated from others with similar interests, and loners alike.

masters...and they love every minute of it. Police K-9 dogs work eight–hour shifts with their masters and never seem to tire. Why? Because they are doing something with the humans to whom they are bonded. So whether you're contemplating a fun activity or a helpful job, find something that can be performed with frequency.

One last item that you should consider is: does this activity require an organization or some other type of support group in order for you and the dog to realize it? For example, field trial dogs must be run

A Miniature Poodle is praised for a job well done after completing an obedience exercise. Photo by Judith Strom.

DOG ATTENTION

Talking about getting dog attention—and you need that before you can teach him anything—reminds me of a funny story an instructor of mine once told me.

There was an old man who had a donkey and a cart. One day he took them up into the mountains and filled the cart with dead wood for his cook stove. Halfway home, with the cart loaded to the brim, the donkey decided to stop. Nothing the old man did could convince the animal to move on.

Finally a young man happened along and asked the old man what he was doing standing in the middle of the road with the donkey and the cart. "Well, I'm trying to get this critter to pull the cart back to my cabin, but he won't budge," replied the old mountain man.

"Well, I might be able to help you, old man," said the fellow. And with that, he walked to the back of the cart and removed from it a long, stout branch. He walked around to the front of the donkey, raised the branch high and brought it down with a crash onto the donkey's head.

"What did you do that for?" asked the surprised old man.

"Well, I'm going to tell him what to do, but first I have to get his attention," answered the fellow.

Teaching a dog a behavior doesn't require you to hit him over the head with a board, but it does require the dog's attention. The dog has to learn to pay attention because he won't be able to remember anything you've shown him if he isn't concentrating on you when you're teaching.

Generally, the more willing a dog is to please and work for you, the easier it is to get his attention at lesson time. Some

This is Carrybrook Jesse James, CD, JH, CGC, a Brittany, heeling in the second level of obedience competition known as the Open class. Photo by Judith Strom.

Before you can teach your dog anything, you must have his undivided attention. Photo by Isabelle Francais.

breeds naturally want to please the owner more than others, but even the most independent dog, regardless of breed, can be taught to give his owner his attention.

There are probably a dozen or more ways to get a dog's attention and the rule of thumb I use is: whatever it takes, providing it's humane, to make a dog pay attention to me is fair. If a dog loves his ball or bone, I use it. I'll show him his toy, then show him a simple behavior and encourage him to copy me. Any behavior, no matter how vague, that comes close to my

desired goal is rewarded with a short, lively game with his favorite toy.

I've taught a lot of dogs to do a lot of things in my years of dog training, and I'm constantly amazed at the variety of things that motivate dogs. I recall training a Springer Spaniel with a duck feather in my hand. A Cocker Spaniel loved to work for a game of fetch with a tennis ball. Hundreds of dogs have learned all sorts of behaviors using food rewards. My own German Shepherd Dog, Morgan, will do anything for a toss of his favorite log of wood that he originally stole off the wood pile in my backyard.

We're talking here about motivation or "heart," as the old timers used to call it long before behaviorists developed a scientific vocabulary for behavior and learning. Regardless of what word we use to describe it, one thing is sure: a dog can be forced to learn a behavior, but he'll never do it happily and reliably if he doesn't have the "heart" for it.

Take a dog with a lot of "heart," teach him to do something, and he'll perform that behavior with a wagging tail all his life. Just talk to people who own dogs and work with them daily—herders, stockmen, narcotics officers, owners of guide dogs, owners of hearing-ear dogs, owners of therapy dogs, law enforcement officers with K-9 dogs—they'll tell you how willingly and well their dogs perform for them every day. Then ask them how the dogs were trained and they'll tell you, "With a great deal of motivation!"

Using your voice effectively, patting the dog briskly rather than rubbing it as in a gesture of love, clapping your hands in applause (dogs love applause!) and talking excitedly using certain words that carry appealing sounds are just some of the

The Open class focuses on more demanding feats of obedience, such as the long sit. Photo by Judith Strom.

Whitestar Bonanza's True Tri, a Papillon owned by DeAnne Erickson, is on his toes and at full attention. Photo by Isabelle Francais.

ways you can motivate a dog.

The best way to find out what motivates your dog is to experiment. Say the dog's name and watch his reaction. When he looks at you, tell him "What a good boy! You're terrific! Oh, I love that! He's such a good boy." Keep your voice high-pitched and happy, and keep talking. Let him realize that responding to his name pleases you greatly.

Wait a few minutes and try it again. If you did a good job of convincing him the first time that looking at you or coming to you when he hears his name is pleasing to you, he'll respond even more quickly the next time. If he ignores you, you probably weren't convincing enough.

In my years of teaching people to train their dogs, the single most difficult thing the people had to learn was effective voice use. However, once they see the positive response they get from their dogs when they "let it all hang out" and get their voices sounding happy, they usually have very little trouble training their dogs. But the initial steps in learning effective voice use usually takes some practice.

If your dog doesn't respond to you the way you'd like him to, don't be disheartened. Work on your voice and don't be inhibited about it. When you see the dog's tail begin to wag as he races toward you, you'll have reward enough to keep on developing a motivational sound that pleases both of you.

Once you perfect your voice you can combine voice use with a favorite object or game and use them both as a reward system for your dog. Remember, your voice will always be with you, so one day you can wean off the motivating object or game and just keep using your voice. By that time, the dog will be conditioned to the behavior and work willingly for a genuine "Good boy!"

Whenever you begin to teach your dog a new

Megan Strom holding a seven-week-old Brittany puppy. Photo by Judith Strom.

Barnard's Yard of Sanshadow, CD, a chocolate Labrador, with proud owner Denise Evans. Photo by Isabelle Francais.

behavior, arrange the lessons at some quiet time and in a place void of distractions. A quiet atmosphere coupled with an enthusiastic owner is the ideal setup for the dog to begin learning, simply because getting the dog's attention will be much easier that way.

Later on, when the dog feels comfortable with his new behavior, you can introduce distracting noises and go to a variety of different locations so he learns that performing his new behavior will occur whenever and wherever you request it, and that it will always produce the praise he needs and enjoys. In other words, he'll have developed "heart" for the activity.

F.E.T.C.H.—Inducive Retrieve Method

Approximately 90% of all chores and fun activities that dog owners teach their dogs are based on retrieving. In other words, the dog must use his mouth to move, hold or carry an object.

There are many ways to teach a dog to retrieve and many of these methods are too harsh, inhumane and/or totally unsuccessful. But many years ago, a friend of mine, Glen Johnson from Canada, devised a way that not only was pleasant for the dog and owner alike but resulted in a high rate of reliability. I have been using the "Inducive Retrieve Method" ever since and with almost 100% success among all breeds of dog, including mixed breeds.

The philosophy of the Inducive Retrieve Method is a simple one: show the dog what you want him to do, give him a reason to do it, and reward him for doing it. Thorndike's Theory that an event that results in a

Playing a game of fetch with your puppy's favorite toy is a good way of teaching him to retrieve. Shar-Pei pup owned by Vicki Hester. Photo by Isabelle Francais.

pleasant consequence will likely be repeated proves itself convincingly in the Inducive Retrieve Method.

Thus **F**un **E**stablishes **T**he **C**orrect **H**abits is an easy way to remember to keep it fun, keep it positive and keep it rewarding.

The method is based on a step-by-step process designed to assist the dog in the beginning and, as he begins to respond to the initial help, to encourage him to assume more and more of the initiative for performing the behavior himself.

Food is the motivator and reward system we use. Therefore, when you begin, it is essential to begin with a hungry dog even if that means fasting the dog one meal before you start. To begin, you'll need:
- •1 chair
- •1 hungry dog
- •1 bowl of nutritious food treats such as cubes of cheese, bits of chicken, beef, pork, etc. (Do not use dog biscuits as they take too long for the dog to chew and swallow.)
- •1 wooden dowel about 6" long and ½ to ¾ of an inch in diameter (depending on the size of your dog).
- •Patience
- •Praise
- •Positive attitude

The best time to begin F.E.T.C.H. training is just before the dog's normal

dinner hour. If the dog is a picky eater, fasting him for one meal before you begin may tip the scales for you: he'll be hungry and alert to the fact that you have a bowl full of food that is obviously for him.

RULES

Never say "No" or scold.

Work only when you are in a positive frame of mind, never when you're tired, angry, upset, etc.

Don't skip steps.

Rest periods should be a

Food is an effective motivator when training your dog. This Vizsla is rewarded for a job well done. Photo by Isabelle Francais.

minimum of 15 minutes with no play and/or petting.

RRP means Remove (dowel, dumbbell), Reward, Praise simultaneously.

THREE PHASES

We will teach retrieving in three distinct steps: Teach the dog to take and out, teach the dog to hold, teach the dog to carry.

Phase I - Take and Out

STEP 1

When teaching a medium-sized or large dog, sit on an armless chair and have the dog sit beside you on your left side (heel position). With a small dog, try sitting on a sofa with the dog sitting on your left. Have the food container on a table to your right in both cases. Allow the dog to see you place a piece of food in your right hand, then let him smell it.

Hold the food securely in the palm of your right hand with your last three fingers. Hold the dowel in your right hand with your thumb and first finger.

With your left hand, reach over the top of the dog's muzzle and, with thumb and second finger, open the dog's mouth just behind the canine teeth using the least amount of pressure necessary. As you do, say "Take" and place

the dowel right behind the canine teeth. Wait two seconds, then say "Out" and Remove (dowel), Reward, Praise simultaneously. Repeat three times.

If the dog actively fights opening his mouth, quit for an hour and try again. As he gets hungrier, he'll become less resistant. In addition, you may have to use his lead (leash) to keep him near you. (Hook lead to collar and place handle end under your feet so as to keep your hands free.)

If the dog resists mildly (he probably will!) by keeping his jaws tightly closed, speak softly, show him the food treat and encourage him to do it "one more time." Be quick with the food reward and praise as soon as you place the dowel in his mouth. (He does not have to keep it there at this point.)

As the dog learns that opening his mouth to accept the dowel results in a food treat, he will become more willing to allow you to open his mouth. When you feel his resistance lessen, you're ready for the next step.

STEP 2

Begin as in Step 1, except you will no longer be forcing the dog's jaw open. Instead, as you command "Take" and present the

In this series of photos, owner Sue Ellen Whitaker teaches her Siberian Husky, Kazakh, to fetch using the Inducive Retrieve Method. Photos by Charlotte Schwartz.

Teaching your dog to retrieve should be a fun experience. This Golden Retriever owned by Pam Blew and Rick Brown can't wait for another chance to fetch the tennis ball. Photo by Isabelle Francais.

dowel by holding it by the end in front of his mouth, brush the dowel gently against the dog's front teeth.

You'll probably see him open his mouth ever so slightly. If he does, praise and repeat "Take" command. Help him by using your left hand to open his jaws wide enough to get the dowel into his mouth. RRP. A few more tries and the dog will be eagerly opening wide enough for

you to place the dowel in his mouth when he hears "Take" and feels it brush against the front of his muzzle.

If he absolutely locks his jaws shut, turns away and refuses to accept the dowel, quit and let him contemplate the food reward he's missing out on. (Generally, the more stubborn the dog, the hungrier he must be to try.) Don't be discouraged. Even the most obstinate dog will come around in a day. Many years ago during a training seminar, Glen Johnson, the famous tracking and scent trainer, told me, "There's no better trainer in the world than a hungry stomach." He was right, and I've never forgotten it!

Once the dog accepts the dowel, you're on your way. And interestingly, the best retrievers are often the ones who put up the most resistance in the beginning! As soon as the dog accepts the dowel, move on.

STEP 3

Once the dog has figured out that treats are the result of opening his mouth on command, he will usually be eager to master this step.

Begin as in Step 1, except do not touch dog's muzzle. Have food and dowel in right hand directly in front of the dog's mouth.

front of and below his mouth. Command "Take." As soon as he does, say "Out." RRP.

Next, lower the dowel to about 4 inches in front of and below dog's mouth. Repeat the process several times with generous praise after each.

Continue to practice, adding distance from dog's mouth until the dowel is resting on the floor in front of him. Keep your right hand next to the dowel, but not touching it.

Now that the dog is picking up the dowel from the floor in front of him, he's ready for the next phase.

Now command "Take" and encourage him to open his mouth and reach forward to slide his mouth over the dowel. Immediately RRP.

You'll notice that as he places his mouth over the dowel, he will close his teeth down on it. Next, he'll probably begin to chew or "mouth" the dowel. For the moment, ignore this—Phase II will address this. Simply remove the dowel as you say "Out." Reward and praise. Repeat three times.

Now begin to present the dowel further away from the dog's mouth. Hold dowel 2 inches in

Phase II - Hold

STEP 1

You and your dog begin as in Phase I, Step 1. Present the dowel at the dog's eye level. Command "Take."

As soon as the dog takes the dowel, place your left hand under his chin or gently around his muzzle if he's really trying hard to spit out the dowel. Say "Hold." Wait three seconds. Say "Out." RRP.

Be sure you don't press his jaws together over the dowel too hard. This will cause discomfort and then he'll never want to hold the dowel.

Repeat until the dog will hold the dowel without "mouthing" for ten seconds. If you wish, you can add "No-chew" immediately after the "Hold" command.

STEP 2

As the dog begins to hold the dowel with a firm grip and without "mouthing," gradually reduce your hand on his muzzle so he will eventually take and hold without assistance or reminders from you. Praise generously always.

NOTE: Mouthing and/or chewing on the mouthpiece are bad habits. If allowed to go uncorrected, they usually escalate until the dog mouths everything he retrieves. By not allowing the habit to form and re-warding a firm grip, you are assuring that the dog will be a reliable, capable re-triever and carrier.

STEP 3

As soon as the dog will take and hold quietly, go back to placing the dowel on the floor and command "Take." As he picks up the dowel, he'll raise his head to face you in anticipation of the food treat in your hand.

Begin to lengthen the amount of time he holds before you take the dowel from him. At first have him hold it for two seconds, then five, then ten, etc. After each hold, say "Out" and RRP.

Phase III - Carry

This is the final and most exciting phase in teaching retrieving. It is

Spencer, a Boston Terrier, races back to owner Joy Parsons with his dowel whereupon she rewards him with lots of praise and a tasty food treat. Photo by Charlotte Schwartz.

usually the one which sets the dog's love of retrieving for all time.

STEP 1

Begin with the dog sitting on your left and you standing. Hold the dowel and food treat in your right hand. Say "Heel" and begin walking with dog on your left. As you do, extend your right hand across your body to a position in front of the dog's nose. Keep walking. Ask the dog "Want this?" and, as you do, wiggle the dowel in front of him so it "comes alive." (Dogs focus on moving objects more quickly than stationary ones.)

In other words, as you and your dog walk along together, psyche up the dog with playful, happy

talk and an invitingly wiggling dowel. When he seems really eager, give him the dowel as you say "Take it."

Once the dog grabs (and he will if you get him really excited!) the dowel from your hand, take three or four more steps, reach down and say "Out." Stop walking as you do and celebrate. (He doesn't have to sit when you stop—concentrate on teaching the carry, not heel and sit at this point.) Just celebrate his amazing achievement—he carried the dowel three or four steps!

STEP 2

Now that he's up, keep him that way. Repeat the exercise and this time, take five or six steps with him carrying the

The polyurethane Gumadisc™ is floppy and soft and is an ideal toy to use for retrieving. The dog bone molded on the top makes it easy for the dog to pick it up when it lands on a flat surface. Photos by Karen Taylor.

dowel. RRP and don't forget to repeat the celebration.

STEP 3

When the dog will take and carry for 15 to 20 steps, he's discovered that he can, in fact, hold the dowel securely in his mouth while he walks with you. Now you can begin to teach him to run out and retrieve the dowel from the floor ahead of you.

As you walk along with the dog at your left side, show him the dowel, wiggle it as before and toss it out three or four feet ahead of you. Say "Take it" in an exciting tone of voice.

The dog will run out and retrieve the dowel before he even realizes that he ran out and picked it up from the floor. Say "Good boy." As he turns to face you in response to your praise, take a few quick steps backward and command "Come." When he reaches you, say "Out." RRP.

STEP 4

Gradually alter your behavior from walking with the dowel in your hand to standing still and throwing the dowel out in front of you. Begin also to increase the distance you throw the dowel. At first it was three or four feet. Within a short time (a few days at most) you should be able to toss the dowel ten feet away.

STEP 5

Now is the time to wean off the food while maintaining your verbal praise and enthusiasm. Instead of having food in your hand, place a piece of food on a low table or chair seat that is beside you on your right. Let him see, but not grab, the food. When the dog returns with the dowel, say "Out," reach for the treat and RRP as you take the dowel from his mouth.

If he drops the dowel before you take it, do not scold or give food. Instead, replace the dowel in his mouth, remind him to "Hold," then RRP. Don't allow your dog to develop the habit of dropping the dowel at his discretion. Use "Hold" to remind him as he comes in to you and slowly build up the length of time he holds it as you begin the final step.

STEP 6

The final step concerns teaching the dog to sit and wait until you send him to fetch and to sit in front of you when he returns with the dowel. Both are easy if you adopt a friendly, helpful attitude. If, on the

other hand, you assume an overbearing attitude, all the fun which you've carefully and methodically built into the work will be destroyed and the dog will no longer work enthusiastically, if at all.

Teaching the dog to wait for the retrieve command requires a delicate balance of firmness coupled with lots of praise and enthusiasm. Have the dog sit at your left side and slip your left hand in his collar. Say "Stay, wait" and toss the dowel. Hesitate three seconds as you remind him to "Wait" again.

If he jumps up in anticipation of running after the

Jennifer Kelly and her mixed breed, Chessie, practice the third phase of the Inducive Retrieve Method—the carry. During her handling of Chessie, Jennifer keeps up a stream of happy, encouraging chatter to help maintain the dog's enthusiasm for retrieving. Photos by Charlotte Schwartz.

dowel, have him sit again and repeat "Wait" while continuing to hold his collar. As soon as you feel him partially relax under your hold, give him the retrieve command. (This can be "Take it," "Get it," "Fetch," or whatever you choose.)

Release your hold on his collar as you send him and praise generously when he returns. Repeat the "Stay, wait, sit" procedure until he shows that he understands that he must wait for the fetch command (he no longer tries to bolt out after the dowel).

Next, place your left hand next to and only lightly touching his neck but not holding his collar. As soon as he will wait without bolting with your left hand near, but not touching, his neck, he's ready for you to stand up straight and simply say "Wait" before you throw the dowel. (The very enthusiastic retriever will probably require a firmer "Wait" than the less motivated or active one. Again, praise both generously.)

When the dog returns with the dowel and is holding it securely, teach him to sit in front of you before you take it from him. As with the previous behaviors, use food for this lesson.

Have a piece of food in your pocket as you send the dog to retrieve. As he's picking up the dowel, place the food treat in your right hand. When he arrives in front of you, remind him to "Hold" and let him see, but not sniff, the treat by slowly raising your hand to at least 12 inches above his head. Do not say "Sit" at this point. (As with other complex behaviors, the dog does not yet realize that he can do two things at once, hold and sit.)

When he raises his head to follow the movement of your food hand, the dowel will roll back toward the rear of his mouth, making it a lot less likely to fall out. Keep reminding him gently to "Hold."

Now slowly move your food hand back toward his shoulders. If your hand is above his head and moving backward, his knees will bend as he continues to focus on the treat. As the knees flex, he'll assume a sit position.

The moment he sits, tell him "Good sit" and RRP. Repeat four or five times and change to a whispered "Sit" as the repetitions proceed.

When the dog begins to retrieve and assumes a sit position in front of you without a reminder, he's ready to do it all on his own with no help from you. Now you're ready to wean off the food reward.

Use a variable-ratio reward system. In other words, vary the times you offer a food reward so the dog never knows when he'll receive food. For example, out of three retrieves, give food for the first and third times. The next session, offer treats for second and third. Next, for the first only.

Praise must *always* be given every time. Even the most enthusiastic retriever will quit if you don't give him a reason (your praise) for doing it.

If the dog's enthusiasm wanes, back up to simpler steps and/or take a day or two off from training. Resume with a hungry dog and *praise*.

CONCLUSION

The whole process of the Inducive Retrieve lesson takes the average dog and owner about one week to learn (that's practicing only a few minutes each day) and one more to perfect. Somewhere along the way, you'll want to exchange the dowel, which by now is probably pretty well chewed up, for a regulation wooden dumbbell.

To the dog, the mouthpiece will feel the same.

However, there will be a wooden bell or block attached to each end. This feature automatically raises the mouthpiece up off the ground, which makes it even easier for the dog to pick up.

If you purchase a quality dumbbell the weight of the added ends will not present a problem to the dog. And if you've taught the dog to "Hold" and not chew or mouth it, the dumbbell will last for years.

As a matter of fact, if you and your dog have done your homework and kept the F.E.T.C.H. in the Inducive Retrieve exercise, you can expect a lifetime of pleasure with a dog that loves to retrieve.

When you are teaching your dog to retrieve, you can use any number of objects. The Gumabone® Plaque Attacker™ is a safe choice. Photo by Karen Taylor.

Agility

Agility. Now here's a sport for dogs and owners that's pure, unadulterated fun for all!

Agility is strenuous activity that turns dogs into athletes while helping them develop physical skills. It can be as simple and inexpensive as teaching your dog to jump through an old tire strung from a tree limb or as sophisticated and expensive as training him to walk planks, climb A-frame obstacles, crawl through tunnels, run a slalom course and even ride a seesaw.

Agility can be performed individually in your home or backyard, at parks with a group of other enthusiasts, or in carefully laid-out arenas where hot competition offers challenges of various levels to dogs and owners alike. In short, it can be easy or complex, whatever you want to make it.

All dogs, from four-month-old puppies to mature dogs, can be trained in agility. There are various levels of difficulty in the training curriculum so dogs and owners can continue to meet new personal challenges each time they reach a given level of achievement.

Not long ago, I attended an agility seminar in San Diego, California. There I watched little puppies as they began to realize that they had two pairs of legs, one in the front and one behind them! And it was fascinating watching them begin to think about what to do with the back pair once they'd set down the front pair while learning to climb a ladder.

At the same seminar, I saw some very accomplished grown dogs negotiate what seemed to be extremely difficult ob-

Leslie Becker and her Norwich Terrier, Ducky, just love agility. Photo by Jenny Eddy.

Jack Russell Terrier, Snowflake, goes up and over an A-frame course as owner Genie Franklin cheers her on. Photograph by Jenny Eddy.

stacles with confidence and joy. They walked across a swaying bridge four feet above the ground and, at the end, ran down a plank and over to the next obstacle, all the while their tails awagging.

Regardless of the level of difficulty, everyone loved what they were doing and seemed reluctant to see it end. What's more, the audience loved it, too!

According to Linda Caplan and Suzanne Clothier, authors of *The Agility Training Workbook*, agility is a sport open to and enjoyed by all dogs, purebreds and mixed breeds alike.

While in the process of training, the owner must take his time in teaching the various agility exercises. Never use force methods and always let the dog set his own pace for advancement and levels of difficulty.

Agility training offers three things to those who become involved in it: fun, confidence-building, and competition. You and your dog can participate in agility in your own backyard just for the fun of it. And that is reward enough to those who make the effort to learn.

But, if you'd like to get into the competitive aspect of the sport, there are two agility groups currently setting the standards for competition in the United States. The United States Dog Agility Association (USDAA) and the National Committee for Dog Agility (NCDA). The USDAA tends to model their equipment after international standards, which are large and not very portable. The NCDA obstacles are "far more portable, smaller, and overall less-demanding equipment."

Both organizations have information on competitive trials, seminars and changes within the sport. Both offer certification following completion of certain performance requirements. Anyone interested in agility for his dog should contact both organizations for additional information and obstacle specifications.

United States Dog Agility Association
Mr. Kenneth Tatsch

PO Box 850955
Richardson, TX 75085

National Committee for Dog Agility
Mr. Charles Kramer
401 Bluemont Circle
Manhattan, KS 66502

Agility Voice
Keba Cottage
100 Bedford Road
Barton-Le-Clay
Bedfordshire, MK45 4LR

Agility Dog Association of Canada
Mrs. Edna Newman
c/o Mallam Kennels
RR 3
North Gower, Ontario
Canada KOA 2TO

Agility work is fun for all dogs and helps them build self-confidence. Here, owner Mike Masters puts Labrador Retriever, Karma, through her paces. Photo by Jenny Eddy.

Standard Poodle, Athena, starts down an A-frame obstacle to join owner Honey Loring who waits at the bottom. Photo by Jenny Eddy.

Coming through the tunnel, this English Springer Spaniel proves that not only is she agile but she also loves new experiences. Photo by Jenny Eddy.

Backpacking

Ch. Uhlan Captain's Cameo owned by Marilee Schafer hits a mountain trail. The backpack consists of two pockets, one on each side of the dog, which can hold a variety of supplies and equipment. Photo by Marilee Schafer.

Here's a rewarding, solitary activity that takes a minimum of training and offers a maximum of pleasure. And when you and your canine companion get away together to savor the great outdoors and taste the peace and quiet of fields and forest, you suddenly realize what a superb relationship this bond between you can be.

Imagine a cool forest floor, the gurgle of a brook falling over rocks, songbirds high in the branches above you, and sunlight slicing through the trees like yellow ribbons strung from a maypole. You walk along, your dog following silently behind. You find your thoughts drifting between the details of your busy lifestyle and the ethereal beauty of this place. Peace descends.

A mile later, you realize this hike, this fresh air, this place where the details of civilization don't matter have lifted you into a state of inner quietude that can be found no other way. And, best of all, your partner shares it with you.

Backpacking is not only good for the body—it's good for the soul.

You'll need about two lessons of 30 minutes each, a few hours of practice in the backyard or a park, and you'll be ready to hit the trail. Equipment is minimal and can be made from things you have at home or can purchase for very little cost.

To begin, you'll need a walking stick, a backpack for your dog, suitable clothes for the outdoors— comfortable shoes are an absolute must—and a plain leather collar with a six-foot lead for your dog.

A walking stick can be anything from a cutoff broomhandle to a pole made from the limb of a fallen tree. It should be about 4 to 5 feet long and approximately 2 inches in diameter. If you make your own from a tree limb, you can remove the outer bark and sand it smooth for even more comfort.

Initially the walking stick will be used to teach the dog to "stay back" behind the handler. Once the dog learns to walk behind the handler, it will prove extremely useful to the handler when out on the trail, particularly over rough terrain and when walking up and down hills, banks and over deadfalls.

The backpack can be handmade or purchased from any of a number of suppliers. The price can range depending on the type of buckles, material, and gadgets the backpack features. To begin, a simple one with a pocket on each side is best. If you and your dog want to go in for distance and long-term hiking, then you can investigate the fancy ones.

How the backpack fits your dog is the most important consideration when you begin. It should fit snuggly yet not bind or cut the dog anywhere. If it does, the dog will be uncomfortable and he'll quit. It should end just beyond the dog's last rib and provide a wide enough neck piece so the weight of the pack is distributed evenly across the dog's front and shoulders.

LESSON 1

The first half of this lesson will be more successful if it's taught in the living room or dining room

of your home. Using the furniture as obstacles, the dog will quickly learn to walk behind you as you negotiate moving in and out among the chairs and tables. Since most of your outdoor backpacking will be done on trails cut through forests or open

With the right planning on your part, a backpacking excursion with your dog can be a highly enjoyable experience.

fields, where the vegetation is tall and thick, he must learn "Back" (to stay behind and follow you rather than walk alongside).

If you're in an obedience class and teaching your dog to "heel" alongside you, he will not become confused between the two behaviors because the command for assuming the backpacking position is "Back." In addition, he'll only receive the command "Back" when you're backpacking and he's wearing a backpack. Shortly, he'll make the association that "Back" is one behavior and "Heel" is quite another.

Fit the empty backpack onto the dog. Then put on his leather collar and lead. Now take the handle end of the lead and tie it around your own waist or attach it to your belt. Make sure that the clasp end of the lead (where it connects to the collar) is under the dog's chin and the other end of the lead comes directly from the center of your back.

Take the walking stick and hold it with both hands across and in front of your body and parallel to the floor so that its ends extend out on either side of your legs in front of the dog's face. It will act as a barrier that the dog cannot pass.

Using the command "Back" to the dog, begin moving around the room in a weaving pattern until the dog learns to stay behind you and demonstrates confidence in his ability to negotiate walking between two pieces of furniture without bumping into them.

Keep praising the dog and reassuring him that his new position behind you is satisfactory to you and worthy of your praise. Use the command "Back, good boy" frequently until he becomes familiar with it, and you see him move behind you each time you say it. Follow that with lots of praise always. Remember that your praise helps build his self-confidence and he will only succeed if he feels sure of himself and what he's doing.

Usually a few minutes of this walking around the house will be enough to get him accustomed to wearing his pack. Next, fill each pocket of the pack with a bath towel or hand towel, depending on the size of the dog and his pack.

Now he'll need to repeat the exercise in the house because, with the pockets full, he'll be wider than he was before and he must learn how to negotiate the

Your dog's backpack, as well as your own, should contain only equipment that is essential for the expedition you are planning.

Even small dogs can go backpacking. A 12-pound Miniature Poodle, Ginger, carries her owner's lunch, car keys, and a dog biscuit for herself in the pouches of her pack. The total weight of the pack should never exceed six percent of the dog's own weight. Photo by Charlotte Schwartz.

furniture with two pockets sticking out from his sides. He'll probably hit the furniture and bump into things at first, but just keep reassuring him and praising with an occasional "Back, good boy."

Once he can handle wearing a full backpack in and around the furniture in a crowded room, move outdoors. Let him follow you across the yard and in and around obstacles so he gets used to working with you anywhere. Always let him wear a full pack with a collar and lead.

Though his pack may be filled with towels, it remains fairly lightweight. As soon as he learns to stay behind you outdoors, add more weight to his backpack. A good rule of thumb for dog backpacks is that the maximum total weight the dog carries should not exceed one-sixth of his body weight. For example, a 60-pound dog can carry a total (backpack and contents) of ten pounds.

During all of his initial training, you should be familiarizing yourself with the use of the walking stick. Learn to move it up, down and sideways in order to keep the dog behind you. Never hit the dog with it, just use it to guide and show him where you want him to stay in relation to you.

LESSON 2

This lesson will begin in the backyard and quickly move to a forest or park trail. For this reason, you will fill the pockets of the dog's backpack with the various items you might want to take on a hike. Items such as a small camera, compass, your lunch, some dog biscuits as treats for your dog, and a plastic ground cover are all things you'll eventually find useful.

Water for you and your dog is essential and can be carried in an army-type canteen over your shoulder by straps. Just be sure you have some way to serve the water to the dog—you can always drink from the canteen.

Balancing the weight of the various items you're packing will be the next tricky part of backpacking. If the backpack is too heavy on one side, it won't sit evenly and the heavier side will constantly be slipping downward as the dog moves, making him most uncomfortable. If this condition persists, the dog will not be able to walk because the backpack will be so twisted around his body and shoulders that he can't walk or it hurts him to do so.

Once the dog feels comfortable with a full pack in your backyard, take to the woods. At first, hike a half-mile and stop for a rest. Remember, if you've hiked a half-mile into the woods, you've got another half-mile to hike going back. If you feel you and your dog can do it, try another half-mile and stop for lunch. Each time you stop, offer water to the dog. When you stop for lunch, give your dog some biscuits. This will make him feel a part of the whole experience and reinforce his love of backpacking.

When it's time to begin the trip back to your car,

Begin acclimating your dog to the pack in your own backyard before going to a forest or park trail. This young Siberian Husky owned by Wendy Willhauck is trying on this backpack for size. Photo by Isabelle Francais.

use the command "Let's go home. Going home, good boy." As you hike along, keep repeating "Home" to the dog and before long he'll learn that "Home" means to retrace your earlier path.

As your experience grows so will your proficiency until both of you look forward to the times when you can get outdoors together and enjoy Nature in all Her glory.

Don't be too eager to take the dog off lead. Allowing him to run free and chase wild animals or annoy others is the quickest way I know to get officials to put up "No Dogs" signs. If, however, your dog is reliable and you're sure he'll stay with you (this could take weeks or months depending on the individual dog), try hiking while you wear the lead as usual and he wears his collar but the two aren't connected. Walk a short distance and, if he stays close behind, increase the length of time he backpacks without the lead.

Eventually he'll stick to your heels like glue and then you'll know you really are a team. However, always have the collar on the dog and the lead on your person in case you meet other people or animals.

Backpacking is a great sport for all dogs and owners, so go for it and enjoy. You'll both be fitter and feel better. Below are some names and addresses for more help.

Alan Riley
6315 North East 196th St.
Seattle, WA 98155

Dorothy Stringer
Route 3, Box 282
Center, AL 35960

Suburban Dog Training Club
4019 Crescent Ave.
Lafayette Hill, PA 19444
(This club has several backpacking members.)

Owners of Malamutes may obtain help and working awards in backpacking from The Alaskan Malamute Club of America by contacting:
Ms. Beverly Hilholland
1210 S. 256th Place
Kent, WA 98032

A letter to the editors of any or all dog magazines may help you locate backpackers in your own area.

Carting

When you find an activity that's both fun and useful, you've really got a good thing going! Of course, carting isn't for every breed of dog, but the big dogs that do it seem to love it. And the owners take great pride in their dogs' accomplishments.

Hauling articles around the yard and farm is an ideal way to utilize the dog's ability to pull a cart. And, for the person who can't use cart pulling at home, there are visits to schools, hospitals, fairs, dog shows and exhibitions where carting is guaranteed to excite a crowd.

Occasionally breed clubs will offer carting classes for such breeds as St. Bernards, Siberian Huskies, Malamutes, Bouviers, Bernese Mountain Dogs, Rottweilers, Akitas, Giant Schnauzers and Great Pyrenees. There are other large, strong breeds that enjoy pulling, too, and if you have a large breed of dog you might consider this activity.

Kimm Pontiff and her Doberman Pinscher, Apollo, take her son Nicholas for a ride down a country lane. In addition to being the resident guardian of the Pontiff home, Apollo also helps haul things around the property. Photo by Charlotte Schwartz.

The AKC can supply names and addresses of some of these groups. Breeders of some of these breeds can often supply detailed information about carting. Some dog supply catalogs offer carts and equipment, and often full instructions for teaching carting to your dog will come with the carts.

One final note: fitting the cart to the dog should be done with the help of an experienced person. Proper weight distribution is the key to success. Without it, a dog finds even a lightweight cart too difficult to pull and he'll quit. In addition, pulling unevenly distributed weight can cause injury to the dog.

The following clubs offer assistance to those interested in carting and draft dog training:

North American Working Bouvier Association
James Engel, President
19007 Millstream Road
Marengo, IL 60152

Bernese Mountain Dog Club of America
c/o Ruth Reynolds
5266 East Fort Road
Greenwood, FL 32443
(This club has information on draft test regulations.)

Newfoundland Club of America
Roger Powell
NCA Working Dog
5208 Olive Road
Raleigh, NC 27606
(You can purchase a complete kit from this club that gives carting instructions, how to start, how to train, and what equipment will be needed.)

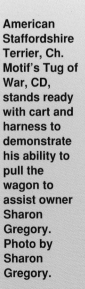

American Staffordshire Terrier, Ch. Motif's Tug of War, CD, stands ready with cart and harness to demonstrate his ability to pull the wagon to assist owner Sharon Gregory. Photo by Sharon Gregory.

These four Basenjis think that their Bernese Mountain Dog friend, Kamali, is great when he takes them for a cart ride. Owner and photographer, Margot Fusci.

Conformation Shows

These shows give the owner an opportunity to exhibit his dog to knowledgeable judges in the hopes that the dog will be judged a good enough specimen of its breed to become a champion. *Note: Only intact (not neutered or spayed), purebred AKC-registerable dogs are eligible for this competition since the purpose of these shows is to demonstrate to the spectators and judges that the dog being shown is considered by the owner to be a superior specimen of the breed and worthy of contributing genetically to future generations.*

In addition to physical conformation, the dog must demonstrate that it has a correct and sound temperament. This is usually done when a judge goes over the dog in the ring and examines it in detail. A sound dog will not show shyness or resentment toward the judge or others in the ring. After all, what's the point in owning a magnificent specimen with an incorrect temperament?

Exhibitors at dog shows must concern themselves with their dogs' comfort and safety. Here most of the dogs are crated while a Standard Poodle reclines on the grass in the shade. Photo by Lynn Updike.

Official greeters at a local dog show, a Shetland Sheepdog and his flag-bearing Border Collie friend welcome spectators and exhibitors alike. Photo by Beverly Walter.

Breeding such a dog would only add a litter of ill-tempered puppies to the world, and the person who truly loves his breed and wants to procreate the best specimens would not sanction the promotion of anything less than the best.

It can take years to learn how to show a dog to its best advantage, but learning by doing and the fun and excitement of winning is the reward one receives for trying. Experienced breeders, breed judges, professional handlers, groomers and other exhibitors all have something to teach the beginning exhibitor. Most are more than willing to share their knowledge and help to launch a newcomer into the sport of showing.

There are classes in

show handling, also. To locate where and when these classes are held in your area, call local kennel clubs and dog training schools. Go to dog shows and ask questions. And in every case, listen. You can call or write your national kennel club and ask them to supply you with the names of places and people who can help you get started.

The American Kennel Club
51 Madison Ave.
New York, NY 10010

The Australian National Kennel Council
Royal Show Grounds
Ascot Vale, 3032
Victoria
Australia

The Canadian Kennel Club
89 Skyway
Etobicoke
Ontario

The Kennel Club
1-5 Clarges Street
Piccadilly
London
W1Y 8AB

Dogs shown in conformation competition are exhibited by breed. Golden Retrievers are judged while at the same time a class of Doberman Pinschers are competing for the all-important points that will eventually earn them the title of Champion. Photos by Charlotte Schwartz.

Finally, you can read. There are a number of good books and magazines available from book stores, book stalls at dog shows, pet shops, libraries and publishers. Just about every breed has at least one book written specifically for and about it. Most of these books are written by experts in the breed and clearly define what comprises a good specimen and how to identify a good dog from a not-so-good one.

The following are periodical publications that are devoted to dogs and dog showing:

American Kennel Gazette
American Kennel Club
51 Madison Ave.
New York, NY 10010

Dog Fancy Magazine
PO Box 6050
Mission Viejo, CA 92690

Dogs U.S.A.
43 Railside Rd.
Don Mills, Ont. M3A 3L9
Canada

Dog World Magazine
Maclean Hunter Pub. Corp.
300 W. Adams St.
Chicago, IL 60606

Off-Lead Magazine *
100 Bouck St.
Rome, NY 13440

* This publication is mainly devoted to dog training. However, it

does contain a schedule of matches, or practice shows, that are conducted throughout the year in most states. It also has classified ads from breeders of specific breeds that might be of help to you.

Show Sight Magazine
8848 Beverly Hills
Lakewood, FL 33809-1604

In England, the following periodicals are available:

Dog World
9 Tufton Street
Ashford
Kent
TN23 1QN

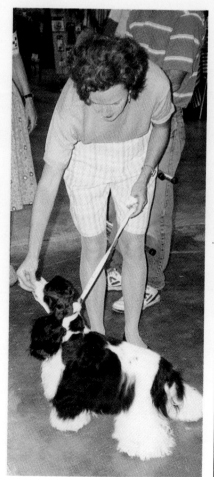

Last-minute grooming and posing are all part of the excitement and anticipation of conformation competition. Photo by Charlotte Schwartz.

Dogs Monthly
RTC Associates
Ascot House
High Street
Ascot
Berkshire
SL5 7JG

Obedience Competitor
PO Box 1013
Thorne
Doncaster
South Yorkshire
DN8 5XF

Dogs Today
6 Station Parade
Sunningdale
Berkshire
SL5 0EP

Our Dogs
5 Oxford Road Station
Approach
Manchester
M60 1SX

Kennel Gazette
The Kennel Club
1-5 Clarges Street
Piccadilly
London
W1Y 8AB

PetDogs Magazine
PO Box B163
Hudderesfield
West Yorkshire
HD4 7YZ

Shetland Sheepdogs waiting patiently for their turn to compete in the dog show ring. Photo by Lynn Updike.

Brothers William and Huston Parsons and their Labrador Retrievers, Wilson and Holly, get off to a good start in the two-mile jog in the Greater Atlanta Veterinary Society's Annual Dog Jog.

speed. As he becomes proficient at it, you can increase the speed to suit his maximum capability. Naturally a large, athletic-type dog is going to be able to run faster and longer than a small one, so always let the dog set his pace.

With few exceptions, dogs can and do love being outdoors and exercising with you. And unlike a lot of people, they don't mind doing it in the wee hours of the morning, when the rest of the world appears to be asleep. Your dog can become the best exercise partner you've ever had!

Field Trials

National kennel clubs provide a wide range of activities for people who own sporting breeds of dog. These breeds were originally bred to hunt and/or retrieve wild game for their owners. For example, the scenting and trailing hounds have activities for their own specialties. Sporting breeds have hundreds of trials and tests in which they can participate, such as hunting and water retrieving tests and trials.

As a matter of fact, in 1985 the American Kennel Club announced a series of new tests for retriever breeds that are recognized by such titles as Junior, Senior or Master Hunter. And no doubt there will be other activities recognized in the future.

This is Fiddlesticks, an English Setter owned by Dr. Terry Terlep, pointing in the field. Dr. Terlep is a well-known veterinarian and field-trial judge.

Spike, a Chesapeake Bay Retriever, learning the ropes at a fun trial. Fun trials are good learning experiences for beginners. Photo by Judith Strom.

Ellie, a black Labrador Retriever owned by Ian Axton, leaps from the bank to begin her swim to retrieve the dummy.

Through the years, I've taught many spaniels, setters, pointers and retrievers on land and in the water. I've also attended upland game and water trials and tests as well as participated in dozens of training sessions. I really can't say which is my favorite—I just enjoy watching people and dogs "doing their thing" together.

Imagine a mahogony red Irish Setter, his feathery tail flying in the wind, racing across an autumn field as he carries a cock pheasant back to his owner. Picture a pair of buff Cocker Spaniels as they flush a quail from a blackberry cover, their cream coats glistening in the late afternoon sun. Or an English Pointer, an alabaster statue, motionless as he points game for his hunter. A short stocky Labrador Retriever, his blue-black coat shimmering over well-developed muscles, as he leaps from a river bank to hit the water below with a splash on his journey to retrieve a fallen duck.

If you're the owner of a sporting dog, it will pay you to look into some of the organized activities designed for your dog. And

Afghans being exhibited at an outdoor conformation show. Photo by Isabelle Francais.

Smart Dogs
PO Box 1013
Thorne
Doncaster
South Yorkshire
DN8 5XF

A final note of caution: many people buy a dog and, some time later, decide they'd like to show it in conformation classes at dog shows. But, as time goes on, they begin to realize their dog isn't a good enough specimen of the breed to be a consistent winner and thereby earn its championship title. At first, they're disappointed and begin to feel that their dog, whom they love and enjoy, isn't worthy of their attention. But sooner or later, they realize that not having a winning show dog isn't the end of the world. They then begin to look for other activities which will involve their dog.

Enjoying the companionship of your dog and realizing that living with him is more rewarding than a few minutes of glory or heartbreak in the dog show ring is what pet ownership is all about. You love your dog and he loves you, and it's within your power to make dog ownership a wonderfully rich experience.

Conformation shows? Give them a try and good luck. But don't forget that there's more to life outside the ring than in it.

Educational and Entertaining Demonstrations

This activity is one which lends itself to dogs with anything from a minimum to a maximum amount of training. Furthermore, you and your dog can offer your services and talents as part of a group or by yourselves to homes for orphaned children, elderly people, children's camps, public and private schools, and rehabilitation centers in your area.

Best of all, you'll rarely be turned down! People are always looking for dogs who can travel and bring a little joy into the lives of others.

The two most important criteria for this activity are friendliness toward other people and mannerliness on the part of the dog. When taking a dog to a facility where there will be children, it is imperative

A small, timid child can learn to enjoy petting a large, well-mannered dog like this Doberman Pinscher, if the dog will lay down for the meeting. Photo by Charlotte Schwartz.

Pet shows and costume contests attract crowds, and dog owners have the opportunity to educate people about living with dogs. Photo by Beverly Walter.

that the dog like young people. Some dogs never have an opportunity to learn how to get along with children, and, if this is the case, the dog should not be forced to interact with them. Children run and squeal and scream and, unless a dog is accustomed to children, the dog should not be exposed to large numbers of them without experience.

In many cases, the dog does not need special training other than basic control. Taking your dog to a retirement home and just walking around to visit the residents can be an exciting event for all. A dog that loves children can visit a classroom for an hour and leave a lasting impression of the wonders of animals with the students.

If you join a group whose

Shopping centers and malls are ideal places for people to become acquainted with dogs. This adult English Pointer demonstrates his ability to watch his owner and sit quietly beside her when she stops walking. Photo by Beverly Walter.

purpose is to give demonstrations and exhibit the dogs in trick routines and advanced obedience training, then you'll need to spend time training your dog. Here you must decide if your dog has the potential to accomplish the lessons and you have the time and motivation to spend practicing. Either way, demonstrations are fun ways for you and your dog to make new friends and bring happiness to others.

One of the most exciting kinds of demonstrations is a dog and handler square dance team. The owners dress in colorful outfits and the dogs often wear bright bandannas around their necks. Then, to country-western songs, owners and dogs perform lively routines led by a "caller." This is a real hand-clapping activity that everyone, participants and audience alike, will long remember.

For more information about demonstrations where you live, contact local kennel clubs, obedience clubs and dog training schools for the names of those already involved. In addition, Therapy Dogs International certifies dogs for this purpose and it would be helpful to contact them as well.

Therapy Dogs International
Elaine Smith
1536 Morris Place
Hillside, NJ 07205

The Delta Society
Century Bldg., Suite 303
321 Burnett Ave., South
Renton, WA 98055
(Both of these organizations can refer you to others who are active in demonstrations and therapy work with dogs.)

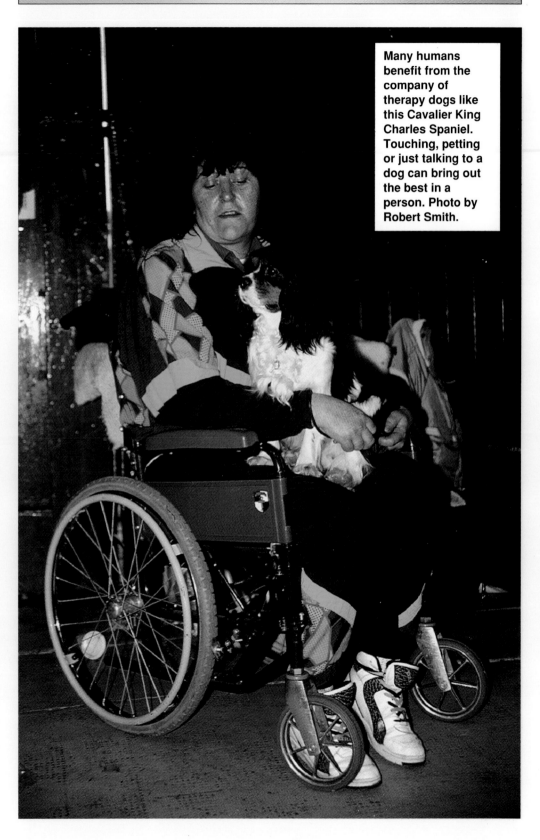

Many humans benefit from the company of therapy dogs like this Cavalier King Charles Spaniel. Touching, petting or just talking to a dog can bring out the best in a person. Photo by Robert Smith.

Exercising—Jogging, Walking, Bicycling

Jogging is good exercise for both man and dog. Here Greta, a Golden Retriever, accompanies Doug Waldorf, her owner, on a morning run. Photo by Charlotte Schwartz.

Stretching and exercising the human body doesn't have to be done alone. There are millions of dogs of every shape and size that exercise regularly with their owners. As a result, both dogs and owners become fit and feel better for the effort.

Puppies and young dogs should not run great distances. Their bones are soft and may not be fully developed until they are one year old or more. Thus, forced exercise can cause permanent damage. So wait until your dog's bone growth is complete and then he'll be able to run circles around you.

Temperature is also an important factor in running. Dogs overheat quickly because they don't sweat like people do. Instead, they pant to lower body temperature, which is less efficient than through the pores as humans do. In fact, you shouldn't run your dog at all during hot weather. In addition, high humidity makes breathing difficult, so if you live where the air tends to be very moist, be cautious. Run when the air is less humid, temperatures are lower and you and the dog feel more comfortable.

When introducing a dog to one of the exercise activities, be sure it's done with the dog on lead. Even if your goal is a fast jog, start out with a brisk

Kimm Pontiff and Apollo, her Doberman Pinscher, take advantage of a beautiful day. Note that they are exercising along a dirt road, which is easier on Apollo's feet than hot pavement. Photo by Charlotte Schwartz.

walk, graduate to a slight jog and build the dog up to the speed and distance that you desire and he can handle safely.

For this, you'll need to teach your dog to heel beside you regardless of how fast or slow you go. Like you, the dog should not have eaten just prior to exercising. And when the dog begins to tire or pant excessively, stop and offer him a few sips (not a bucketful!) of water from your canteen. Build up his stamina gradually and even the smallest dog will become an athlete. Of course, expecting a Chihuahua to run 26 miles is out of the question, but if

Small dogs as well as large dogs can enjoy jogging. Owner Joy Parsons displays the Frisbee won by Spencer, her Boston Terrier, at the Seventh Annual Dog Jog in Atlanta after they completed the one-mile jog.

The Greater Atlanta Veterinary Society holds an Annual Dog Jog in Piedmont Park. Hundreds of dogs and people turn out to participate. Photo by Joy Parsons.

Even small dogs can enjoy bicycling. This is the author and her Miniature Poodle, Ginger, starting out on a five-mile ride. When carrying small dogs in baskets on bikes, make sure that they are securely attached so they can't jump out. Photo by Yvonne Gamblin.

you're reasonable and the dog is in good health, he should be able to keep up with you for several miles without any problems.

One of the most important things to remember when teaching a dog to run beside you, whether you're on foot or wheels, is to be aware of the terrain under the dog's feet. Blacktop, cement and coarse sand can injure the pads of his feet. Soft sand found along country roads and grass are ideal. However, broken glass and debris on the shoulder of the road are dangerous.

Salt, used to melt snow and ice on highways in the cold regions of the country, can burn the dog's feet severely. If a dog's feet are injured, and he associates the hurt with the activity, he may quickly decide he doesn't like this type of activity and refuse to accompany you. But worst of all is the suffering of the animal.

Once the day's exercising routine is finished and you're back home, let the dog cool down for an hour before offering him his meal. Feeding a dog large quantities of food right after strenuous exercise can cause severe digestive problems, even death. So a few sips of water to wet his tongue and a period of rest will assure you a healthy, happy partner who'll be fit and eager to go out with you another day.

In the case of bicycling, be sure the dog is kept on a long enough lead to allow him to run either alongside or behind the wheels. If he gets too close, the wheels may run over his feet and he'll shy away from the bike in the future.

In the beginning, ride slowly and encourage him to set his pace to your

one of the bonuses can be making new friends along the way (some of my dearest friends are field trialers!).

Write to the American Kennel Club or your national club for details. They can supply you with names and addresses of clubs and individuals in your area as well as a copy of the rules and regulations for trials and tests for your breed. See the *Gazette*, their monthly publication, for listings of trial sites and dates.

The American Kennel Club publishes a free quarterly newsletter for those involved in field trials. To receive a free copy write to them at:

The American Kennel Club

Attention: David Savage
51 Madison Ave.
New York, NY 10010.

For owners of bird dogs, there is the Bird Dog Foundation. In their museum, they've identified almost 40 different breeds of dogs, many AKC-recognized, used in the sport of birding. They publish a periodic newsletter and will gladly send you additional information upon request.

The Bird Dog Foundation, Inc.
PO Box 774Y
Grand Junction, TN 38039

For all other types of sporting dogs, try to look up local kennel clubs and field trial clubs. See your

Mystic Rail's Shotmaker, an English Pointer owned by Dr. Terry Terlap, poses on point during a recent hunt. This typical pose indicates to the owner that the bird dog has located a covey of quail in the underbrush. Photo by Marilyn Terlep.

Golden
Retriever
owned by
Kathy and
Ted McCue
retrieves a
duck. Photo
by Isabelle
Francais.

phone directory under "Dog Clubs" and "Kennels." You may also be able to find monthly magazines and periodicals sold at newsstands. Another way to get involved in dog sports is to check out the dog training clubs and schools in your area. And of course, breeders of your particular breed of dog are a valuable source of information.

Go to dog shows, trials and matches in your area. The only way to find a particular activity that interests you is to actually see it. At first, you may want to investigate sports that your breed of dog actively participates in and excels at. For example, Labrador Retrievers have always dominated field trials. However, do not limit yourself to only those activities—try to see as many different trials and matches as possible to find one that is suitable for both you and your dog.

You should also talk to local veterinarians, trainers and instructors. They usually know dozens of people who are active in dog activities.

Brittany
retrieving a
Chukar
pheasant.
Photo by
Judith Strom.

Chesapeake
Bay Retriever
retrieving a
pigeon.
Photo by
Judith Strom.

Flyball

Here's a sport that provides exercise and good fun for dogs and excitement for spectators as well as owners. The object of the game is for the dog to run out to a box, step on a lever that releases a tennis ball into the air, retrieve the ball, and race back to the owner. In addition, there are a series of low jumps over which the dog must jump on his way out to and back from the box.

Played alone it's fun and exciting, but played as part of a relay team racing against another flyball team as originally developed, the sport provides even more excitement.

In her book, *Flyball: A Dog Sport for Everyone*, author Lonnie Morgan explains it this way:

"Flyball is a relay race between teams, each with four dogs and four handlers. Each one of the dogs takes a turn at running over a course of four jumps with a flyball box at the far end. The dog depresses a pedal on the front of the box, which in turn releases the throwing arm sending a tennis ball into the air. The dog catches the ball and runs back over the course across the finish line at which point the next handler lets his dog go. The first team to have all four dogs successfully complete the course is declared the winner of that heat."

If you have a healthy dog that's physically

Ann Legare and her Welsh Springer Spaniel learn Flyball. Photo by Jenny Eddy.

capable of retrieving and jumping low hurdles, your dog can learn. Instructions for teaching flyball and information about the newly formed North American Flyball Association can be obtained by writing to:

Lonnie Morgan
5307 W. Grand Blanc Rd.
Swartz Creek, MI 48473.

Above: Blaze, a German Shepherd Dog, jumps over the hurdles and gets the ball by himself as his owner waits for him at the starting line. Photo by Jenny Eddy. *Left:* In Flyball, the dog must step on the pedal in front of the box, which, in turn, releases a tennis ball into the air.

Frisbee®*

*The trademark Frisbee® is used under license from Mattel, Inc., California, USA.

Would you like to teach your dog to play Frisbee®? You can, you know.

Frisbee® is another activity that's fun and great exercise for both you and your dog. And, best of all, you won't need a support group to enjoy it. The old game of catch has been revitalized, and now you and your dog can play catch with a flying disk in your own yard, a park, or anywhere you can find some grass or soft ground.

The dog will quickly learn to leap into the air and snatch the flying disc that you've thrown for him. Once he learns that maneuver, you can teach him to bring it back to you for another toss.

I know of several very enthusiastic Frisbee®-playing dogs who seem to never want to quit. They absolutely love it .... and so do their owners.

In addition, there are now competitions throughout the United States where you and your dog can demonstrate your expertise and possibly win a prize for your efforts.

As always there are a few

Frisbee® is an activity that is fun for both owner and dog. Photo by Robert Pearcy.

Dogs love to catch moving objects and Frisbee® is the perfect game to get their attention and incite their chase instincts. The polyurethane Gumadisc® is so soft that it doesn't hurt you, your dog, or the window is might strike accidentially. Photo by Isabelle Francais.

exceptions to the "every dog can play" theory. Certain breeds are far too big-boned and heavy to go taking flying leaps in the air. For them, the consequences are usually injury to legs, hips and back. There are also dogs that have back problems, hip joint abnormalities, even knee disorders. These dogs are candidates for lots of other fun activities, but not frisbee. So be sure your dog is physically sound and capable of playing before you attempt to teach the game.

For the dogs who are physically suited and agile for frisbee, there are specially designed disks from Nylabone. The Nylabone Frisbees® are constructed of chew-worthy nylon, making them stronger than the original

Frisbee®. The Gumabone® Frisbee® has a bone molded on the top to make it easier for the dog to pick up.

By writing to the addresses below, you can obtain free booklets to get you started:

In addition, you can get a list of available books, video tapes and related products by requesting the "Flying Dog 1995 Products Guide" from the Atlanta, GA address below.

Come 'N Get It Canine Frisbee® Championship
Dept. DF
4060D Peachtree Road
Suite 326G
Atlanta, GA 30319

How To Teach Your Dog To Catch a Frisbee®:
Gaines AWI Booklet
PO Box 8177
Kankakee, IL 60902.

Kimm Pontiff and her Doberman Pinscher enjoy a game of Frisbee on a summer day. Photo by Charlotte Schwartz.

A Collie owned by Lori Tackabury with a Gumadisc™, a specially designed disc from Nylabone® that is constructed of chew-worthy nylon making it stronger than the original Frisbee®. Photo by Karen Taylor.

Herding

Ch. Kifdehoup Noir, UDT, a Belgian Sheepdog owned by Augusta Farley, rounds up a flock of sheep in a pasture on a ranch outside Santa Fe, New Mexico. Photo by Augusta Farley.

If you are the owner of one of the many herding breeds of dogs, here's a scene you might like to consider: Picture a great green valley surrounded on all sides by tall, rugged mountains. You are standing high up on one of the bluffs looking down on the valley. It's early in the day and the sun is washing the valley in bright yellow light. Below you see what appears to be a huge undulating blanket of light-beige fluff. Then you realize that the blanket is, in fact thousands of sheep all clustered together and flowing across the valley floor. You wonder what makes them move. Certainly it isn't the shepherd or his helper who stand off to one side and observe the process from a distance. Then you spot three black specks that constantly circle the moving herd. Closer examinations reveal the specks to be small black and white dogs. These are Border Collies, and it is they who drive the herd for the shepherd from

This is Serena Natural Attraction, a Shetland Sheepdog owned by Linda Zimmerman, with a pair of Nubian goats. Photo by Isabelle Francais.

one end of the valley to the other. While doing so, they also keep the sheep from panicking and separating into small groups.

Later that day you talk to the shepherd. He tells you how these three dogs regularly move thousands of sheep from one valley to another, through narrow streets of small towns and down dusty roads past moving vehicles and strolling people.

And they do it every day of their lives. They're born to herd, and Border Collies are probably the best herders of all the herding breeds in the world today.

We're not suggesting that you turn your personal pet into a full-time herding dog. Rather we're offering another hobby which might prove of interest to you and your dog.

All across America there are herding trials open to all the herding breeds. Usually there are five or six sheep which must be herded from one location to another, through a variety of realistic obstacles such as fence gates.

These trials are conducted by various breed clubs in some instances and by the American Kennel Club in others. There are four basic levels of achievement which encompass herding instinct, herd control, cutting out specific sheep from the herd, and even a championship level.

Genevieve Cameron gives a lesson in herding to her German Shepherd Dog, Timee's Cinderella. Using her staff, Genevieve guides the dog in circling the sheep as they move from one pasture to another.

Preparing a dog for competition in one of these trials requires a dedication to training, physical conditioning, and patience in obtaining control of the dog from great distances. It is not something achieved quickly or without sacrifice, but it is a wondrous reward when accomplished by both dog and owner.

If herding competition sounds like something in which you and your dog might be interested, there are several steps you can take to acquire help and information.

Write to the American Kennel Club, 51 Madison Avenue, New York, NY 10010 for their *Herding Book of Regulations*. There is no charge to pet owners for this pamphlet.

The American Kennel Club also publishes a free quarterly newsletter for those involved in herding. To receive a free copy write to them at:

The American Kennel Club
Attention: David Savage
51 Madison Avenue
New York, NY 10010.

The following clubs can be contacted for additional information about trials and training:

Australian Shepherd Club of America, P.O. Box 921, Warwick, NY 10990.
American Border Collie Association, Rte. 2, Box 255, Perkinston, MS 39573.

Most breed clubs that sponsor trials open their entries to all herding breeds so you need not have a dog of their breed to obtain information or to participate. If that is the case, these clubs may be able to refer you to others in your area and with your own breed of dog who can assist you. In addition to the breeds of the Herding Group, the Rottweiler (a member of the Working Group) may also participate in herding trials due to the breed's herding/droving-dog ancestry.

Additionally, the American Kennel Club may be able to refer you to clubs in your area so ask when you write for their publication.

Left: Australian Shepherd performing a herding instinct test. Photo by Judith Strom. *Below:* Border Collie rounds up a flock of sheep. This breed is probably the best of all herding breeds in the world today. Photo by Robert Smith.

Home Helpers

This category can include anything and everything from bringing in the morning paper to warning you of strangers at your door to fetching his own leash when it's time to go out. Actually this category is limited only by your own imagination and your dog's capabilities. Because home helpers can be so multi-talented, I will list a few jobs here to get you started in thinking about ways your dog can help you around the house.

Alarm dogs usually evolve rather than develop through formal training.

Example: someone knocks on your door, your dog barks and you respond. After this has occurred several times, your dog learns that when he hears a strange sound at the door, he can get your attention if he barks. As he matures and becomes more attached to you and his home, he begins to react more reliably to a variety of strange sounds—whether they come from a person knocking on the door or a prowler in the yard.

Some dogs are naturally more protective than others. Large breed dogs have

These two Boxer puppies are helping with dinner. Breeder, Richard Tomita. Photo by Isabelle Francais.

deeper voices that don't carry as far as the higher pitch of the little dog, but their weight and size alone is often enough to discourage strangers from intruding.

The incessant sound of a little dog barking, however, is often enough to discourage unwanted visitors. Someone intending to break into your home does not want to draw attention to himself or the house. Either way, dogs in general are usually very effective, self-appointed guardians of their homes without a lot of formal training.

Teaching your dog to bring in the morning paper is helpful to you and fun for the dog. Begin with a lightweight section of newspaper rolled up and se-

cured with a rubber band. Once your dog learns to pick up the newspaper and carry it a few feet to you, you'll be ready to increase the distance he carries it. Have him bring it to you in another room. Then make the distance two rooms. Finally, when he's loving the work and eager to retrieve it, place the rolled-up section outside the front door and have him bring it through the doorway and into the house.

If the dog is likely to run away or play a "catch me if you can" game with you, keep him on a long line so he can't run away as he fetches the paper from the yard or front porch. With a slight bit of pressure on the other end of the line, encourage him to come to you with the paper and reward him with a big celebration when he does.

Once the dog is comfortable with carrying one section of newspaper in his mouth, you can begin to increase the weight by adding another section every few days until he's able to carry the entire issue. Just be sure he can physically handle the total weight of the paper. For example, a tiny breed will find it impossible to pick up a Sunday edition of the average newspaper.

Training a dog to perform any chore or behavior should be done in slow, easy steps. Make sure the dog understands what you expect him to do, show him that he pleases you by praising enthusiastically, and proceed to the next level of difficulty only when the dog demonstrates that he understands the work and is eager for more. This is the basic formula for successful training regardless of what you're teaching. And it ensures success for both you and the dog.

Some other jobs that you might consider teaching your dog to perform around the house are: bringing a bag filled with dirty clothes to the laundry room, helping to carry a basket of cleaning supplies from room to room as you dust, etc., putting away his own toys into a box or basket at the end of the day (have you ever noticed how easily he takes his toys *out* of their resting place in the morning?!), carrying your keys to the car, carrying bags of groceries into the house when you go shopping, and finally, bringing you his empty food dish after he's eaten his meal.

As I mentioned earlier, these are just some ideas you may want to think

First thing in the morning, Emma, a Standard Schnauzer, fetches the daily paper for owner Marilee Schafer. Photo by Marilee Schafer.

You can teach your dog to pick up after herself. Ginger, the author's Poodle, is busy collecting her toys and putting them away for the night. Photo by Charlotte Schwartz.

about once you've decided to teach your dog to help make your life a little easier while providing fun things for your dog to do. I am, however, sure that your own imagination will provide you with a whole collection of ideas even more suitable to your lifestyle and circumstances.

Whatever you decide, enjoy your dog and his learning.

This Golden Retriever is cleaning up his Nylabone® toys after a day of fun. Photo by Karen Taylor.

Jumping

Teaching a dog to jump is not unlike teaching a boxer to fight in the ring. It takes months of learning how to use his body followed by many more months of repetitive, consistent conditioning to turn out an athlete that can use his body effectively to negotiate whatever obstacles he must jump in order to perform a task or compete in one of a number of athletic sports.

"Oh, but my dog already knows how to jump," you say. "He jumps on the sofa a dozen times a day."

A dog that jumps up and down stairs, on and off furniture, in and out of an automobile, or on and off your lap is not necessarily an athlete. Furthermore, if your dog is similar to most modern-day dogs, he probably spends the major portion of his time in passive activities, such as watching people stroll past his window, watching you move around the house, reclining on the backporch steps in the sunshine, etc.

We refer to these types of dogs as "natural" jumpers. In other words, they jump simple hurdles that are present in their particular

With his bright red sweater and flying ears, Gemini Olympian, Am. UD, Can. CDX, a Cocker Spaniel, sharpens his expertise at the broad jump. Owner, Sandra Meade.

Puli clearing the bar jump at an agility trial. Photo by Karen Taylor.

environment in order to achieve a specific goal, such as getting up on the sofa. Through a method of trial and error, they taught themselves to hurl their bodies from one place to another to satisfy some need or desire.

Another way of thinking about it is to say that anybody can pop another person in the nose, but that doesn't make him a boxer. Boxers are athletes. So are dogs trained to jump.

And similar to the process of turning an ordinary man into a professional boxer, there are many aspects of canine jumping that must be considered

and addressed before a dog becomes an accomplished jumper. For example, we must know the speed of the dog's movement when approaching a hurdle, the height and depth of the obstacle itself, the footing before and after the jump, the dog's physical condition and abilities. Finally, we must have a plan as to how we're going to motivate the dog to jump.

The consequences of an inadequate approach to teaching the dog to jump correctly are twofold. First, he may not become a successful jumper and lose confidence in his ability to jump. Once the dog discovers that he lacks the skills

Right: A Poodle jumps through several hula hoops on a fun day at the park. Photo by Lynn Updike. *Below:* Marsh Dak's Shooting Star, CD, a black Labrador Retriever owned by Dianne L. Schlemmer, leaps over the obedience bar jump. Photo by Karen Taylor.

to negotiate a hurdle, the motivation to do so dies.

Second and more importantly, the dog is likely to injure himself in his attempt to please his owner and jump. Injuries in jumping can be as minor as a bruised foot or hock or as devastating as a spinal injury, which could cause permanent impairment in normal activities such as walking and running. Unfortunately, many of the latter type injuries are accompanied by a lifetime of pain and/or discomfort.

In short, teaching a dog

to jump is a serious under-taking and should never be approached casually. Instead, it should be done under the guidance and instruction of a knowledge-able trainer who is experi-enced in the art of canine jumping.

The flip side of the coin is great excitement and plea-sure for the dog who learns how to jump properly and loves jumping, plus the pure joy for the owner who appreciates the perfor-mance of his athletic ca-nine companion.

There are many repu-table obedience clubs, schools and classes throughout America that have at least one instructor in the organization who is well versed in teaching jumping. One way to find out if there is a group in your own area that offers this training is to look for dog classes in the Open

Above: This Doberman Pinscher shows off his jumping skills at an agility trial. Photo by Karen Taylor. *Left:* Vom Vilhaus Ram, Am. and Can. UD, a German Shepherd owned by Ed and Flo Wilson, sails over a 34-inch high jump at a trial to thrill spectators.

A Dalmatian gracefully leaps over the brick wall at an agility trial. Photo by Karen Taylor.

and Utility level of obedience training. (These two levels of obedience training require jumping.)

The American Kennel Club's *Obedience Regulations Book* gives some valuable information on jumping heights for all breeds of dogs and suggested construction measurements for three different types of jumps, the high jump, the broad jump and the bar jump. This book is free by writing to the AKC at 51 Madison Avenue, New York, NY 10010.

Don't try this at home. Professionals can train stunt dogs to perform supercanine feats. This talented and fearless German Shepherd jumps through a hoop of fire. Photo by T. Buckley.

Lure Coursing

Ginger, a
yellow
Labrador
Retriever
owned by
Zalie Liun,
spots the lure
in the grass
as it whirs
past her.
Since the
lures usually
are set to
move quickly,
the dogs
should be in
good physi-
cal condition
before racing.

Sighthounds such as Afghans, Greyhounds, Ibizans, Borzoi, Salukis and Whippets have been bred for centuries to run and catch game, particularly hare. In some countries of the world, where the hare is an important source of food, sighthounds are still used for this purpose.

In the United States, running wild game has been translated into a popular sport known as lure coursing. It uses the dog's natural instincts without involving the killing of game.

In lure coursing, a prede-termined course, marked by large wooden spools spiked into the ground, is set out in an open field and a light monofilament line is strung in the grass from one spool to the next. A motor-driven plastic rabbit is then set in motion over the course just ahead of the dogs so they can chase it. The speed of the rabbit is determined by the speed of the dogs running it, i.e., the faster the breed, the faster the rabbit moves so that it stays just ahead of the quickest dog in the race.

The American Sighthound Field Associa-

tion is the guiding organization in the United States for lure coursing. Though there are no schools that teach lure coursing, coursers who are active members of ASFA are always seeking newcomers who are interested in running their dogs.

Sighthounds can be introduced to lure coursing when they are a few months old by tying a rag on the end of a long string and dragging the rag over the ground. When they see beginner dogs because it teaches them not only to chase the lure but also to run with other dogs and not become distracted by or aggressive toward the other dogs.

From running my own Ibizan Hound in lure coursing trials, I can tell you that watching sighthounds race across a field after a plastic rabbit is a thrilling sight. And where the race course is hilly, it's so exciting to see the pack one minute as

The swift moving Sloughi has been trained to course a variety of game including rabbit, gazelle, and coyote. Photo courtesy of Mosica Arabians.

the rag move through the grass, their natural instinct will activate and they'll chase the rag all around the yard.

As they get older, you can take them to lure coursing practice sessions. There they will have the opportunity to run with other puppies. This is excellent experience for they gallop across a field and then watch as they disappear from sight when the "prey" dips into a valley. Moments later, your heart skips a beat when you see them reappear up over a hillside as they race down the final stretch of the course.

Once the dogs reach the end of the course, they are

met by their owners and praised enthusiastically. If you have a sighthound, this is a very exciting hobby for both of you.

For more information regarding lure coursing and a list of those who can help you in your area, contact:

American Sighthound Field Association
PO Box 1293M
Woodstock, GA 30188

Gary Forrester
2050 Theion Dr.
York, PA 17404

Bunny Reed
RR 3
Ogden, IA 50212

Sighthounds, such as Pharoah Hounds (above) and Whippets (below), are excellent coursing dogs.

Chasing a mechanical bunny around a manmade track has alleviated the senseless killing of rabbits on public fields. Lurcher photographed by Isabelle Francais.

Judi Roisland
PO Box 405
Grasonville, MD 21638

Arnold Ross
4333 Mt. Jeffers Ave.
San Diego, CA 92117

Susan Stafford & Kathy O'Brien
805 Hillside Blvd.
S. San Fransisco, CA 94080

Don Wilson
Rt. 1, Box 237
Blythewood, SC 29016
In addition, the American Kennel Club publishes a free quarterly newsletter for those involved in lure coursing. To receive a free copy write to them at:
   The American Kennel Club
   Attention: David Savage
   51 Madison Avenue
   New York, NY 10010.

Obedience

Initially people enroll themselves and their dogs in an obedience class in order to train the dog to obey, develop a repertoire of good manners and build a bond of companionship with the owner. Upon completion of the original eight-week course, some owners decide that they and their dogs have done reasonably well and enjoyed learning together. They then become motivated to seek additional training.

A second, third and even fourth course of study proves so successful and enjoyable to both dog and owner that the owner decides to take up obedience trialing as a hobby. In other words, they've been bitten by the bug and they join the ranks of thousands of dog and owner teams who compete on a regular basis for obedience titles.

As stated in the AKC *Obedience Regulations Booklet* under the heading of Purpose, "Obedience Trials are a sport and all particpants should be guided by the principles of good sportsmanship both in and outside of the ring. The purpose of Obedience

A group of owners and their dogs are receiving awards for jobs well done in an obedience competition show. Photo by Genevieve Cameron.

Trials is to demonstrate the usefulness of the purebred dog as a companion of man, not merely the dog's ability to follow specified routines in the obedience ring ..... the basic objective of Obedience Trials is to produce dogs that have been trained and conditioned always to behave in the home, in public places, and in the presence of other dogs."

There are three basic levels of achievement that, when successfully mastered, can result in the dog earning a special title. For example, the first level is called Novice and can result in the words "Companion Dog" or "CD" placed after its name.

Level Two is called Open and the title earned in that category is "Companion Dog Excellent" or "CDX." The most difficult level of achievement is called Utility and results in the title "Utility Dog" or "UD" and finally "Utility Dog Excellent" or "UDX." When a dog reaches the level of "UD," he can then be entered for competition in Obedience trials where he will compete with other "UD" dogs.

After the dog has successfully completed all the requirements of the Obedience Trial Championship level, the letters OTCh. will precede his name. This is the ultimate goal of the true obedience competitors and it can

These young dogs began Kindergarten Puppy Training when they were two or three months old. Now, eight weeks later, they celebrate graduation. Photo by Charlotte Schwartz.

Top: Owner Dee Julian teaches her Shar-Pei, Sadie, to walk in a figure 8 pattern. This exercise will help the dog to change pace as the owner does. Photo by Charlotte Schwartz. *Below:* An overview of the 1992 Gaines Cycle Eastern Regional Dog Obedience Championship held in Gainesville, Florida. Photo by Lois Wenner.

take anywhere from two to six years to obtain.

Precise descriptions of all exercises required in all levels plus complete instructions of how each of those exercises is scored can be found in the AKC *Obedience Regulations Booklet.* You may obtain a booklet by writing to the American Kennel Club, 51 Madison Avenue, New York, NY 10010. The book is free of charge to dog owners.

One of the definitions of the word "sport" is a pleasant pastime or recreation. The sport of dog obedience provides much more than that. It can open up a whole new world of dogs and people to the participant. You can travel to

Uhlan Matter of Record, CD, and owner Judy Bard receive their well-earned green ribbon from Judge Mayborne for qualifying at an obedience trial. Jason, as he is known to family and friends, earned three green ribbons and was then awarded a Companion Dog title by the American Kennel Club.

different towns, even states, to compete. You'll meet people from a wide variety of backgrounds who all share your enthusiasm for the sport.

After a lifetime of being involved in the sport of dogs, much of which was in obedience trialing, I count about 85% of my many friends around the world as originating from one or more dog activities. In other words, dogs and the people involved with them have provided me with a rich, full life of experiences and friendships that I would never have had if it had not been for them.

If you would like to get started in the sport of dog

Dogs in a Novice Obedience class practicing the sit/stay exercise. They learn to sit and wait patiently without moving while their owners walk away and return to them one minute later. Photo by Charlotte Schwartz.

Zelda, a Doberman Pinscher, sails over a bar jump during a practice session for an obedience trial competition. Owner and photographer, Lois Wenner.

training and obedience, seek out a dog club in your own area. Enroll in an obedience class under an experienced instructor who is known for using humane training methods and has a good record of success with students, both canine and human.

In addition, reading a variety of training books written by knowledgeable and experienced instructors can give you a broad range of methods for teaching your dog each and every exercise required for the various levels of achievement. You'll find that not every method works identically for each dog, so opening your mind to a selection of ideas will arm you with the necessary skills to teach your dog and help him enjoy the learning.

Top left: Champion Motif's Thief of Hearts, an American Staffordshire Terrier, demonstrates his high jump skills, which helped him to earn a Companion Dog Excellent title from the American Kennel Club. Owner and photographer, Sharon Gregory.
Top right: Joy Parsons trains her Boston Terrier, Spencer, to come. Photo by Charlotte Schwartz.
Below: Vom Vilhaus Sieben, a German Shepherd owned by Ed and Flo Wilson, practicing his broad jump. He was an American and Canadian Utility Dog and Obedience Trial Champion in both America and Canada.

Scent Work

Teaching a dog to use his nose can include everything from having him find "lost" toys to lost people and/or felons, to drugs, weapons, insects, and escaping gases. In this book we will discuss how to teach the dog scent work to find things and people around the home for fun. Teaching such types of scent work as narcotics detection requires a much more sophisticated level of training and is usually done by professionals.

A dog discriminates different scents with his nose much the same way people discriminate colors with their eyes. Therefore, if a dog were to smell a pot of spaghetti sauce simmering on a stove, he would identify it (if he could talk) as tomatoes, oregano, oil, onion, and the various individual ingredients that went into making the sauce. Man, however, would merely sum it all up by saying he smelled spaghetti sauce cooking because it's infinitely more difficult for him to isolate

Golden Retriever participating in a scent discrimination exercise in obedience competition. Photo by Karen Taylor.

Scent work can be useful in narcotics detection. A Labrador Retriever searches a suitcase for drugs in this public demonstration. Photo by Isabelle Francais.

the various scents of all the ingredients.

Because a dog's nose is thousands of times more sensitive than a human's, he finds it quite easy to discriminate different smells. He can, for example, learn the difference between the scent of a plastic container and the scent of a bone. In addition, he can easily be taught the difference between the scents of two people since each of us carries our own unique "scent print."

Try hiding his favorite toy, let's say it's a ball, under the corner of a sofa pillow. When you begin, ask him, "Where's your ball?" and gently lead him toward the sofa. With your hand make a slow, sweeping motion across the seat and stop at the pillow that hides his ball.

Keep talking and getting him curious about finding his ball as you pick up the pillow corner so he gets a whiff of the ball. As he recognizes his toy, praise him and let him have it. If you are excited enough and he enjoys the game of hide and seek, he'll quickly learn to identify his toys by name and seek them out in different places. Before long, you'll have a trick that he willingly performs for family and guests because, to him, it's another game he loves to play with you.

When you begin teaching him to find various members of the family, teach him the person's name as you ask, "Where's Suzie?" (or whatever the person's name). Have the person sit in another room and gently guide him to that room.

When he sees Suzie, be sure Suzie praises him for "finding her" and have her call him to her. The next time, have Suzie in a different room, but this time, have her sit off in a corner rather than out in the middle of the room. Don't have Suzie hide completely just yet.

Repeat the procedure, making sure to help the dog by getting excited and repeating your question, "Where's Suzie?" Go with him and, if he seems confused, use your hand and make slow sweeping motions within the dog's scenting range (usually that should be about two to three feet ahead of him when he's just learning scent work). Slowly move around the room so the dog learns to cover an entire room and not just the center of it. When you and the dog arrive at the place where Suzie is sitting or standing quietly and he discovers Suzie, join in the celebration of his "find."

As soon as the dog gets the idea of using his nose to locate a person, have the person hide in a closet. However, in the beginning of this stage, leave the closet door ajar to make it easier for him to find the person. And, of course, a big celebration must follow each "find."

As the dog's proficiency increases, you can make the game more difficult by getting the target person (Suzie) completely out of sight. Once this occurs, you'll really be able to observe the dog using his nose instead of his eyes to find his person. For example, if the person is completely hidden in a closet, you'll notice the dog sniffing the air at the bottom of the closet door and becoming more excited in his effort to tell you he's found Suzie. He may whine, paw at the door, bark, even turn excitedly in circles. Any indications he gives you that he's located the person who is hiding should be recognized and praised by you.

Once he's told you by his behavior that the search is over, you should open the door and go with him to greet his hide 'n seek friend. Then the three of you should celebrate his achievement together. Remember, your dog is playing this game because he's learned to enjoy the attention it earns him and the togetherness he gets from being with you.

Now that you've got the dog scenting to locate known (to him) people, you can graduate to teaching him to find objects for you. However, before you can do this, you must teach him to take (pick up), hold and carry things in his mouth.

Let's say you'd like to teach your dog to find your car keys. (For the habitual car key misplacer, this can be a welcome relief to an irritating problem!)

First, teach him the name of the object, in this case, "keys." Play with the keys, throw them on the floor and encourage him to retrieve them for you. Let him become accustomed to the smell of metal and the feel of metal in his mouth. Always keep it a game and always celebrate when he fetches them for you, even if he drops them later. His F.E.T.C.H. lessons will teach him how to hold on to objects and carry them long distances.

As you did when you taught him to find Suzie, make the hiding places easily accessible to him such as under a piece of paper on a low table, tucked under the corner of a pillow, in a shoe on the

Teach your dog to find a favorite person. First, lead the dog into the room where the person is hiding. In this case the woman is in the closet. A few sniffs at the door will convince the dog that her friend is hiding behind the door. The treat in the woman's hand is a further reward for the dog when she makes the correct decision. Photo by Charlotte Schwartz.

floor, etc. Remember that when you misplace your keys, they're not usually hiding in a closed closet or a dresser drawer. They're simply resting wherever you put them down when you walked into the house.

When the dog can find the keys and retrieve them, have him bring them to you in various rooms of the house. If you have two stories to your home, expand his retrieve distance to carrying them up and down stairs. Soon you'll have a partner who'll never again see you searching frantically for your lost keys!

Finding car keys is just an example of what your dog can be taught to do if you'll take the time and make the effort to teach him. I know of at least a dozen golfers who have trained their dogs to locate and retrieve golf balls in the tall weeds and grasses of a rough. And in the doing, these dogs save their owners a lot of money in what would otherwise be the cost of lost balls!

The more he learns, the better he'll be at everything he does because he loves working with you. So use your own imagination to find things he can do with his incredibly powerful scenting ability.

The dog finds her friend in the closet and is rewarded with a treat. Repeat this process and soon the dog will learn to search even harder because she has learned that a warm greeting and a treat are in store when she succeeds. Photo by Charlotte Schwartz.

Schutzhund

Schutzhund originated back in the 1800s as a proving ground for canine intelligence and temperament levels. Today in America it is a sport for some of the large working dogs and their owners.

Doberman Pinschers, Rottweilers, German Shepherd Dogs, Giant Schnauzers, Belgian Sheepdogs, Belgian Tervurens and other breeds of similar types are usually the dogs trained in the sport of Schutzhund.

The word "Schutzhund" is of German origin and means "protection dog." In that context, there are three categories or branches of Schutzhund work: Tracking, Obedience, and Protection Training.

Within each of these categories there are three levels of achievement, Levels I, II, and III. Governing the sport throughout the country is Schutzhund U.S.A., an organization that awards the various titles to dogs having earned passing grades at each level. Once a dog starts in Schutzhund training, he is given a record book that stays with

him throughout his career and is the official document of his individual performance and achievements.

For obvious reasons Schutzhund work is not a sport for every dog and/or every owner. It requires both to be of sound mind and strong physical ability. It requires a dedication to perfection of performance, a ruthless ability to recognize flaws and weaknesses in the dog, and an untiring willingness to work with others in the sport, both dog and human, to prove the value of each dog to be precisely what it was bred to be when its breed was established.

What's more, Schutzhund work is hard work requiring hours of physical effort in training, practicing, and testing.

The dogs are trained to move among a crowd of chattering people without getting frazzled. They learn to stop a fleeing felon and back off when told by their owner. They must learn to search blinds for felons in hiding, then warn their owners of the presence of that felon without attacking the suspect. They must demonstrate their proficiency at basic obedience both on and off lead, and finally they must learn to track a human scent to

Schutzhund demonstrations are always crowd pleasers. Law enforcement officers use the opportunity to educate the public about the purpose of Schutzhund training. Here two officers and their dogs wait to give a demonstration at a shopping mall. Photo by Beverly Walter.

Top: A padded canvas cover is used to protect the "suspect's" arm from being bitten. Generally in training, each officer acts as a suspect for another officer's dog. *Below:* Upon verbal command from the handler, the dog must release his hold on the suspect and return to sit beside his handler without being physically restrained. Note that the handler is not even holding the dog's leash. Photos by Beverly Walter.

lead their owners on the path of a person who has gone before them minutes or hours before.

Once they learn these and many other behaviors, they must then prove themselves in a series of tests before some of the toughest judges in dog sports. Only then are they awarded the famous Schutzhund I, II, or III titles.

Though Schutzhund training in America is considered a sport, it is nevertheless a serious sport and one not meant for every dog and/or owner. Whenever we deal with protection work in dogs, we must hold the highest regard for the dog's ability to inflict damage on other dogs and people. Thus, those who are considering Schutzhund work as a potential sport should be guided by those experienced in the field.

If you'd like to contact someone in your own area who may be able to give you additional information on the sport, you can reach the parent organization by calling

Schutzhund U.S.A.
Phone: 314-894-3431.

Owner/handler Augusta Farley works with Aaron von Breuker Heide, her Belgian Malinois. Heide demonstrates her Schutzhund expertise as she heels alongside Ms. Farley during a training session. Heide has earned a Schutzhund III title, which indicates her high level of control. Photo by Loving Photographic.

Sled Pulling

Dog sled pulling can be a very simple or very complicated sport for man and dog alike. It all depends on how involved the owner wishes to become.

In its simplest form, a dog is taught to pull a sled across the snow. The dog is fitted with a good harness and the weight of the sled is the initial resistance he'll feel. Once he becomes accustomed to having a sled dragging behind him, additional weight can be added in the form of articles or a small child. If the dog is big and strong, he can be taught to pull the weight of a man with no problem.

In its more complicated form, sled pulling means the dog runs with other dogs as a team and pulls large, heavy sleds which usually carry equipment and a person.

Sled dog racing is a very popular sport in the northern part of the continental United States, Alaska, and Canada.

The best known dog sled race in America is called the Iditarod and is held annually in Alaska.

The race covers over 1,100 miles of rugged terrain from Anchorage to Nome.

Races can be a few miles to many hundreds of miles long and last for days. During this time, dogs and drivers race, eat, and sleep out in the wilderness in sub-freezing conditions. Teams that participate in this type of racing usually practice most of the year in preparation for these events which, incidentally, often award large sums of money as prizes.

When there is no snow on the ground, the teams frequently pull sleds rigged with wheels in forests and conservation areas of state and national parks. Dog

Jacqueline Fraser and Joyce Bradley will ride in the sled while the driver will stand behind on the runners. Photo by Charlotte Schwartz.

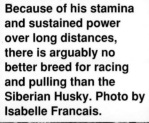

Because of his stamina and sustained power over long distances, there is arguably no better breed for racing and pulling than the Siberian Husky. Photo by Isabelle Francais.

In the little town of Frisco, Colorado, high up in the Rocky Mountains, a team of dogs is getting ready for a fun run through snowy mountain trails.

sledders routinely devote weekends to traveling around with their teams and competing at local levels as well as national ones.

This sport is not one in which a dog and its owner should participate alone. For obvious reasons, there are far too many risks for a dog and its owner to be out in the wilderness without the benefit of others when something goes wrong.

For more information and help, contact:

International Sled Dog Racing Association
Box 11
Bakers Mill, NY 12811

Northern Dog News Magazine
6436 Mullen Rd.
Olympia, WA 98503

Team and Trail Magazine
Center Harbor, NH
03226

Down East Sled Dog Club
Kathy and Grey Pickett
RFD 1, Box 3261
Mechanic Falls, ME
04256

New England Sled Dog Club
Arlene Sylvester
12 Heath Street
Newton, NH 03858

Sledding is an exhilarating sport for participants and spectators. Photo by Isabelle Francais.

Christmas 1987: the Von Bruka Rottweilers out with their sleds in the snow. Owners, Bruce and Karen Billings.

Sports—Camping, Hiking

There are quite a few sports, some of which you may already be practicing, in which you can involve your dog.

For example, I know of many people who are avid golfers. When they play alone or practice, they bring their dogs along to retrieve the balls. The exercise and togetherness are excellent for both humans and dogs.

If you're a golfer, you may want to consider this idea. With a little patience and effort, the two of you will have a regular routine going and you'll both enjoy it.

Thousands of dogs go camping with their families every year. Although dogs are prohibited in some state parks, there are many private campgrounds that allow dogs providing they are under control at all times.

It's important to respect the rights of others and never allow a dog to bark unnecessarily or relieve itself without the owner's picking up after it. This is simple, common courtesy and if dog owners will think of others when they bring their pets into public places, then the public will not ban dogs from recreational areas.

As for the dog, there are a few considerations to think about when you take him into the outdoors. Always apply a bug spray or rub-on stick to prevent him from being bitten by insects. And remember that a dog needs access to shade and water, so take the time to provide his necessities and comforts and he'll enjoy the experience as much as you.

When a dog swims in brackish, cedar or salt water, he needs to be rinsed off with clear water at the end of the day. His skin will react to the minerals in anything other than pure water and that, in turn, will cause itching, which leads to secondary infections. After all, you rinse the swimming water off your own body, why not off your dog's?

When we think of dogs hiking, we think of foot problems. Too many pet owners take their dogs hiking without giving thought to the dog's comfort. Sharp articles such as broken glass, jagged edges of cans, sand burrs, and prickly vegetation bruise and injure the pads of the dog's feet.

In addition, walking on the hot tarmac of country roads in summer can burn the pads of the feet. Keep your dog on the soft shoulder of the roadway and watch carefully for any foreign matter that may be lodged between the toes.

When hiking, watch the dog to be sure he doesn't get too tired—fatigue causes accidents in man and dog. Stop and rest frequently and you'll get a lot more miles for your effort than if you plow on unconcernedly.

As long as you're hiking,

Swimming is an integral part of camping. Cole, a Labrador Retriever, retrieves a Frisbee thrown into the lake by his owner. Photo by Zalie Liun.

Hiking over hills and valleys is healthy and pleasant for owners and dogs alike. Here Afghan Hounds, Brando and Maxwell, take a rest at mid-point in their hike with their owners. Photo by Jenny Eddy.

you may want to consider teaching your dog backpacking. That way, he can carry his own food as well as some of your equipment.

If the outdoors and the company of others like you appeal, try a doggie camp such as Camp Gone To The Dogs in Putney, Vermont. Owner Honey Loring offers two one-week sessions in late June and early July each year. Campers and their dogs stay in regular rooms of a private boarding school and enjoy gourmet meals in the school dining room.

Activities are so varied that it boggles the mind and creates lasting memories of the most unusual vacation a dog and owner can share. In addition to enjoying the scenic beauty of southern Vermont's Green Mountains, campers participate in such diverse activities as herding, agility, obedience, retrieving, flyball, frisbee, sled pulling, costume parties, softball, swimming, hiking and carting.

You can obtain a brochure with complete details by writing *Camp Gone To The Dogs*, Honey Loring, RR 1, Box 958, Putney, Vt. 05346. You'll find her extremely knowledgable and enthusiastic, a true dog lover who has created one of the most unique opportunities for dogs and owners we've ever seen.

Participate with your dog in sports—you'll both be happier!

Taking your dog camping can be a rewarding experience for both of you. Be sure to provide food, cool and clean water, and shade for your companion. Photo by Jenny Updike.

Tricks

There are quite a few good books written exclusively for teaching your dog tricks, so we will not repeat those instructions here. However, lets look at some of the types of tricks people

All-American dog, Dusty, loves to perform tricks with his owner, Zalie Liun. Here Dusty jumps over his owner's back on command. Photo by Honey Loring.

teach dogs.

Simple tricks are usually those that most people have seen dogs perform and always bring forth a smile and a round of applause from the viewers. One-late night television show has, for years, promoted dogs and their owners doing tricks and it never fails to bring on enthusiastic audience reactions.

Tricks include shaking hands (paws), sitting up and begging, speaking, rolling over, playing dead, saying prayers, smiling on command and singing. Most dogs can be taught all or some of these tricks. And if taught motivationally, the dogs love to perform them.

Basic tricks such as these usually consist of one or two behaviors which the dog can accomplish with little or no help once he's mastered it. And if there are children in the family, dog tricks can provide hours of lively entertainment for kids and dogs alike. In addition these types of tricks are always winners if your dog is a therapy dog.

More complex tricks are a challenge and a source of great pride when learned. Behaviors such as taking an object to another person, jumping over and/or through an object, finding an object among a variety of other objects by name, finding an object by scent from among a variety of similar-looking objects, retrieving a variety of objects on command from various places, answering a ringing telephone and carrying the receiver to the owner, learning to distinguish colors and interacting with other animals are all complex tricks.

It should be pointed out that, due to breed, size, age and/or physical ability, not every dog can be taught every trick. Therefore, you need to study the behavior under consideration very carefully before attempting to teach a dog any trick. All these behaviors and many more take great patience, effort and time to teach. Once accomplished, however, they're worth all you and the dog put into it.

Since many tricks re-

quire the dog to take, hold and carry an object in its mouth, it is important that you first teach your dog to fetch before you try to teach him any tricks.

Local pet shows usually offer prizes to dogs who perform tricks. Here are two examples of what you can teach your dog to do. *Above*: **Dog and owner dancing.** *Below:* **Dog playing dead. Photos by Lynn Updike.**

Terrier Hunting Field Trials

The hunting instinct of terriers remains strong today and is evident even in puppyhood. Here four Cairn Terriers are hunting. Photo courtesy of Chris Carter.

The American Working Terrier Association holds field trials for all AKC- and UKC-registered terrier breeds that are bred to follow game into the ground. The association recognizes the following breeds as earth breeds of the correct size and character to hunt underground: Australian, Bedlington, Border, Cairn, Dandie Dinmont, Fox, Lakeland, Norwich, Norfolk, Scottish, Sealyham, Skye, Welsh, West Highland White, Jack Russell, Patterdale Terriers and all Dachshunds.

In these events the dogs go to ground in long tunnels to reach a rat that is caged and protected from being captured by bars at the end of the tunnel. There are three levels of expertise for the canine entrants.

Junior Hunter earth trials involve tunnels about ten feet long and include one bend. Senior Hunter earth trials have 30-foot-long tunnels and include three bends.

The Master Hunter level is even more advanced and requires the dog to find his way through a complex pattern of turns including false (unscented) tunnels. After "working" the quarry, the dog is then required to respond to his handler and retreat from the tunnel, a behavior that is very much against the dog's wishes.

In all levels the dog is expected to "work" the rat at the cage for a minimum of one minute in an attempt to get the quarry. In the first two levels the dog is removed from the tunnel via a trap door just above the rat's cage. In the Master level, the dog must

come out himself.

A good working terrier can be clearly heard above ground as he barks incessantly while trying to get at his prey. With many dogs, it's more difficult to get them out of the tunnel than into it. Being ratters, they quickly learn that this sport is what they've been bred to do and they hate to give up without getting those "little varmints."

In addition to underground trials, the American Working Terrier Association also offers above-ground field trials. In these events, the trials consist of a maximum of seven tests.

Dogs receive individual certificates for each test. The categories include obedience control, scent trailing, land retrieve, water retrieve, gunshot and pack temperament.

If you have a terrier or Dachshund and think you'd be interested in letting your dog participate in a sport that utilizes his natural instincts, contact The American Working Terrier Association and they'll put you in touch with others in your own area. And if your dog does well, he'll be awarded a well-earned certificate.

The American Working Terrier Association
Gordon Heldebrant
2406 Watson Street

Patterdale Terrier works a hide on a wheel during a training session. Photo by Isabelle Francais.

Sacramento, CA 95864
Phone: 916-485-5950

In July 1994, the AKC introduced Earthdog Tests and offered three new titles: JE, SE and ME. These new titles indicate that the dog has passed the required tests for Junior Earthdog, Senior Earthdog, and finally Master Earthdog. These tests are similar to those offered by the AWTA and are executed in a like fashion.

Karla Martin
4013 County Line Road
Southington, OH 44470

Therapy Dogs

Dogs are being used regularly for all kinds of human therapy and, what's so wonderful about this new aspect of human health care is that the dogs are creating some remarkable results. Autistic children, for example, who can not or will not speak to anyone, now find they can relate and talk to dogs. Once the barrier of silence is broken, they go on to communicate to others.

Elderly people, people who have to learn to speak all over again because of strokes, people who are recuperating from serious injuries, mentally handicapped people and people with serious emotional problems are communicating with dogs. And, once they begin to do that, they proceed successfully up the ladder of recuperative steps in preparation for rejoining society.

There are therapy dogs that visit homes and hospitals weekly or monthly for a few minutes. There are therapy dogs that live in institutions and become

A visit from a friendly Cocker Spaniel brings joy and excitement to this elderly nursing home resident. Photo by Joan Adams.

part of the lifestyle of the residents there. Frequently, they're something in between: their owners pay regular visits to institutions (many residents develop their favorite therapy dogs and ask to pet and hold them each time the dogs visit). All of the dogs socialize, some perform tricks while others demonstrate obedience routines and special skills. All are welcome.

Some owners take their dogs to schools to help educate children in the care and training of dogs. Many of these owners also introduce the children to cats, rabbits, gerbils and other small pets. Teaching children how to be caring and kind to animals is the beginning of teaching them how to be caring and kind

to their fellow humans. Thus the children grow up to be more sensitive to the needs and concerns of others.

Taking dogs into prisons and juvenile detention centers has proven beneficial to the residents in many ways. Like the children in schools, they learn about animal behavior and that violence is dangerous not only to their adversaries but to themselves as well. In addition they discover that violence and abuse never solve anything. Instead they learn there are many acceptable ways of getting along with others. They begin to communi-

Therapy dogs are welcomed visitors at many hospitals and nursing homes. Photo by Joan Adams.

Sue Ellen Whitaker training her Siberian Husky, Kazakh, to jog alongside her husband's battery-powered scooter. Kazakh is learning to stop and sit when the scooter stops at intersections and never to pull when the cart is in motion. Photo by Charlotte Schwartz.

Kazakh, a Siberian Husky, sits on command to receive a treat from his owner, Sam Whitaker. Photo by Charlotte Schwartz.

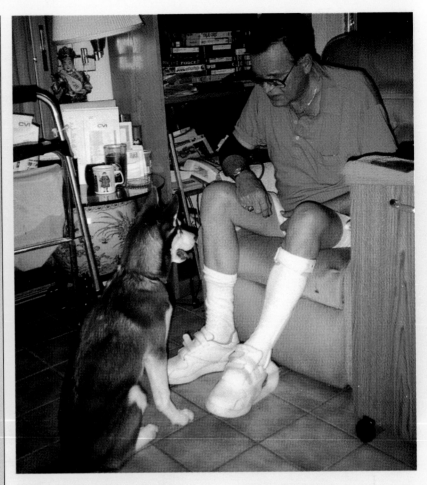

cate. And, through the dogs, they build self-esteem, the first step in discovering self-worth.

Whatever your circumstances and your goals for your therapy dog, you can be sure that your pet is doing so much more than just being a lovable addition to your life. He or she is making a valuable contribution to the quality of life for mankind.

For details and additional information on how to get your dog involved in therapy work, contact:

Delta Society
Century Building, Suite 303
321 Burnett Ave.
South Renton, WA 98055

Therapy Dogs International
91 Wiman Avenue
Staten Island, NY 10308
(Therapy Dogs International certifies dogs for this work.)

NOTE: Many humane societies have therapy dog programs and are always looking for volunteers, so check these organizations in your area.

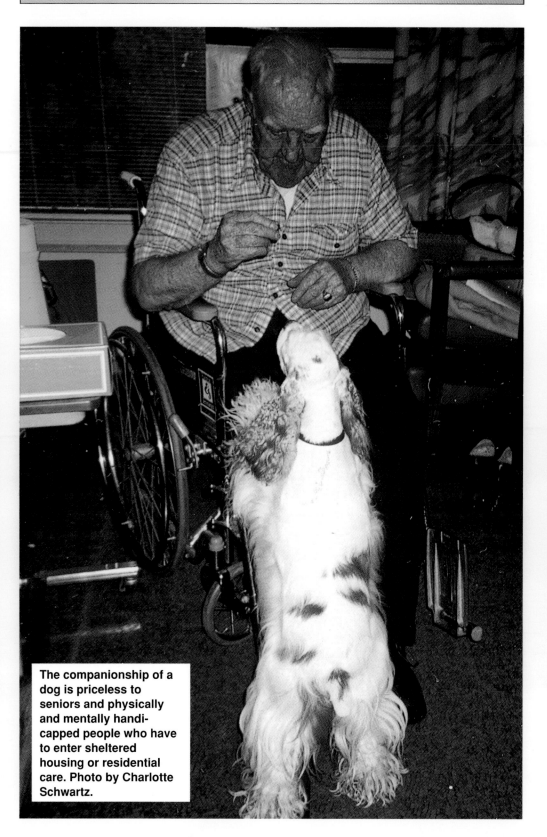

The companionship of a dog is priceless to seniors and physically and mentally handicapped people who have to enter sheltered housing or residential care. Photo by Charlotte Schwartz.

Tracking Trials

Tracking Dog (TD) and Tracking Dog Excellent (TDX) titles are awarded by the American Kennel Club to dogs that have demonstrated to the judges that they can follow the path of a person who has gone ahead of them minutes or hours before. And when the dog is tested, the tracklayer is nowhere in sight.

At the end of the track, the dog must indicate a dropped article, usually a leather glove, that the tracklayer has left behind. The difference between the two titles is the degree of difficulty of the tracks, such as age and distance. In addition, a TDX dog has learned to distinguish between a track laid by one person versus track laid by a diversionary person called a cross tracklayer.

All dogs can learn to track, though some are better than others. All AKC-registered dogs can earn a TD. It isn't difficult to teach a dog to use his nose, but it takes a long time and miles of walking to teach an owner how to "read" (understand) his dog and go with him when the dog's behavior says, "He went this way, boss." However, it's one of the most thrilling moments in life when a dog passes a tracking test and earns that coveted TD.

Come along with me on a verbal tracking test and I'll try to share with you the thrill of what I call "the loneliest sport."

Dogs of all sizes can learn to track. Chris, a Shetland Sheepdog, leads owner Jean Trapani along the track. Photo by Honey Loring.

Owner Perry Nelson and Katie, his Golden Retriever, start out for a day of track training. The beginning of the track will be marked by the two flags and will help Perry determine when Katie locates the start of the track. Photo by Honey Loring.

It's early morning, long before the sun considers it decent to rise, on an autumn day. You've driven for two hours to arrive at the test site on time. All the while you've been driving along the deserted freeway, your dog has slept peacefully in the back seat. Only your mug of coffee and the hope that you two will pass the test today has kept you going.

An old farm house and an open barn with several sleepy people standing around greet your arrival. You notice the horizon in the east is beginning to lighten up. Dawn.

A short time later, you and your dog are driven to a large field where you're told that your test will be conducted "out there." You look for starting flags, the only clue of track direction you'll receive throughout the entire test. Nothing.

Then, off to your left and alongside a dirt road cutting through the fields, you spot two flags with small red banners flipping gently in a breeze that's just begun to kick up. "You'll be starting from those flags in about ten minutes," remarks one of the judges.

Your stomach twists and

flags now. Angel, a 12-pound Miniature Schnauzer, is wearing her leather harness, and you're trying desperately to look composed as you untangle the 30-foot nylon line that connects the two of you like an umbilical cord.

Angel puts her head down and sniffs the area around the first flag. You stand back, trying to stay

Olympia, a Standard Poodle owned by Honey Loring, stands between the two flags of a track attempting to determine which way the tracklayer went.

squirms into a knot, your dog wags her tail at the handful of people standing around. Suddenly you're not at all sure you should be here, but you've worked hard and paid the entry fee, so you reason that you might just as well give it a try. This won't be the first time Angel's made a fool of you, you remind yourself.

You're at the starting

calm, trying to keep your mouth shut while she studies the scents on the ground. Sure, you're allowed to speak to the dog during a tracking test, but too much talking can distract her and cause her to miss a turn or get off course. After a year of practicing together, you believe you've learned through trial and error when to speak and when to keep quiet and let Angel work things out for herself.

Suddenly, Angel begins to move out away from the flags and you feed out the line until she's about 20 feet ahead of you. Then you fall in behind her. Your eyes are glued on that little ball of gray with the stub tail that wags ever so slightly when she's on track. You watch for signs.

Before you know it, she stops dead in her tracks and picks up her head. Track's gone. She's lost it. One minute she was on it and following confidently. The next, she indicates there's no track. What can you do? Nothing. Let her work it out. Relax. Remember, in this sport, the dog leads, you follow.

She circles wide around you and you turn slowly to keep the line from tangling. You ask, "Where is it, girl?"

There! She pulls hard to

Bulldog being started on a track. Photo by Robert Pearcy.

the left and, nose down and all business again, she signals you to follow. You do.

But just when you think things are going well, she stops again. You check the direction of the now brisk breeze and remind yourself to relax. She's done all right up to now. Leave her alone and let her do her thing.

This time Angel indicates a turn to the right. But, you note, there was no circling. Just a sharp turn, her nose still on the ground and a firm pull as she throws her tiny body into the harness. . .

Something in the back of your mind says, check the wind. Sure enough, you're heading straight into the wind again and you realize Angel didn't have to circle. She picked up the new leg of the track as it blew directly toward her. She's an efficient worker, no need for unnecessary circling. Let's get on with the job, she says. I want to find that glove.

You may be dying a thousand deaths out there, but Angel's having a wonderful time. She loves tracking, and despite her diminutive size and short legs, she's got all the heart in the world. And that's what gets her through. It's a good thing, too, because while you follow along, a

million thoughts flashing through your mind, Angel disappears before your eyes! The field cover has changed from short to tall and Angel is somewhere down there at the bottom of all that tall grass. Only the taut line in your hand tells you she's still working and on track. No slack, no hesitation, no circling. Just a hard pull from an invisible little dog racing through a field with an owner following blindly along.

Quickly, you glance around. In the distance you see one of the judges standing on a dirt road off to your left. Though he's too far away to see it, you know there's a whistle hanging from a rope around his neck. Silently you pray he won't blow it for that would indicate that Angel is lost and you've failed the test.

Your thoughts are interrupted again when Angel stops and the line goes slack. What seems hours later, you watch as the line tightens again and begins turning in a wide circle. She's still working. Though you can't see her, you realize she's telling you there must be a turn here and she's trying to locate the track's new direction.

In your most confident voice (please don't let her know how nervous I am!),

The Bloodhound is a renowned tracker and sniffer. Photo by Isabelle Francais.

A Basset Hound being introduced to the scent of the article that it must track. Photo by Vince Serbin.

tighter and tighter and you pick up your pace in order to keep up. Angel must be running now, you think. Oh, please let her be right, you say aloud.

All of sudden, you realize the second judge is 50 feet behind you. Your heart thumps loudly. Clipboard in hand, he watches stone-faced as you begin to jog.

Angel keeps going. This leg must go on forever, you think. When is she going to slow down, you wonder? It seems an eternity that you've been out here in this field. And despite the chill in the air, you don't feel a thing.

But before you have time for any more thoughts, the line slows and loosens slightly. It doesn't stop, just eases off a bit. You watch and feel intently for any sign she'll give you.

Another turn? Lost track? Unexpected distractions? What? "Speak to me, Angel," you implore silently.

A sudden quick jerk on the line and a pull to the right tell you to be on the alert. Something's changing out there. If only you could see her, you might be able to help.

Then the line goes dead. Your heart really does stop this time. You've got to move up the line. Maybe you can get close enough to see what she's up to.

you ask once more, "Where is it? Where's that glove? Go find it, girl."

Suddenly she does. She pulls hard to the left. You feel the line tug in your hands. Your eyes strain for a glimpse of your little partner, but there's nothing to see. The cover is too thick and too tall. All you can see is the line as it moves between your fingers and you feel her saying, "Follow me! I've found the new leg."

You do. Once more, the dog has things under control. You pray she's right and the dreaded whistle won't blow.

But you don't have time to worry now. That line gets

Maybe now you can help.

No use. It's too late. Without any more warning than a slack line followed by a tug, you watch as the line begins to curl back toward you. She's given up, you think. She's lost the track and she's coming back. We've blown the test. Your heart sinks. After all these months of training and now it's over.

Over, indeed. As Angel cuts through the grass and races toward you, you see what you never expected to see. She's carrying the glove! She found it!

As she arrives, you drop to your knees, open wide your arms just as you've done a hundred times before and scoop her up. "Good girl," you cry, tears rolling down your cheeks in unashamed joy.

She drops the glove, licks the tears from your face, and wiggles free. She picks up her prize and races around you in circles as if to say, "Look what I found! Now let's play!"

The judges arrive at your side. You stand up and everyone hugs everyone. "Congratulations," says Stone-face. "That little dog ran a fine track, and you did a good job of handling, too."

In the distance you hear the small group of other trackers and tracklayers cheering you and Angel. Then you realize they'd been watching all along. The judges leave you and Angel alone. There are still more tracks to run and they don't want them to get too old. Time is important.

Special K Skipper, a German Shorthaired Pointer owned by Delwood Miller, following a track. Photo by Karen Taylor.

Making it all look easy, this Golden Retriever is AmCan. OTCh. Culynwood's Buckthorn Taiga, TD, WC owned by Judy Myers.

You remove Angel's harness, roll up the line and say, "Let's go back, pretty girl. I've got some breakfast waiting for you."

Lonely? You bet! It's the loneliest feeling in the world to be out in the middle of a 40-acre field knowing that only your dog knows which way to go.

Exciting? Absolutely! The thrill of putting all your faith in your dog after months of training together and following blindly along until that moment when your dog reaches down and picks up a leather glove cannot be adequately described on paper. Only those who have walked those miles, who've gone home wet and cold and exhausted and filled with doubts, who've trained through the stages of trying to catch birds and butterflies and follow gopher holes down to China, who've learned to trust their canine partners when it comes to scent work, will ever know the thrill of earning a Tracking Dog title. It truly is one of life's most exhilarating moments.

Angel stops and looks up at you. You toss the glove and let her retrieve it again and again. After all, this moment is what she worked so hard for. This is her moment of glory, too. You look around and see the judges and the group moving on to the next test.

In the United States there are quite a few tracking clubs that offer support, help, and, in some cases, even lessons.

But without a group to help, an owner and dog can accomplish it alone. We did.

What you can't do without, though, is a book of instruction to give you specific lessons and a booklet of rules and regulations from the American Kennel Club if you want to enter tracking tests.

Listed below are important names and addresses for would-be trackers.

Tracking Club of Central Florida
1820 Harrel Rd.
Orlando, FL 32817

Hudson Valley Tracking Club
17 Palma Blvd.
Albany, NY 12203

Midwest Tracking Association
1470 Elizabeth St.
Glendale Hts., IL 60139

Lenape Tracking Club of Central New Jersey
PO Box 326
Lebanon, NJ 08833

Buckeye Tracking Club
60 E. Catawba Ave.
Akron, OH 44301

Gateway Tracking Club
20 Steeplehill Lane
Baldwin, MO 63011

Indian Nations Tracking Club
25931 Lariat Circle
Broken Arrow, OK 74014

Tracking Club of Massachusetts
PO Box 56
Ayre, MA 01432

Western Carolina Tracking Club of Tryon
RD 2 Box 119A
Fletcher, NC 28732

Above: Prunella Williams and her Cocker Spaniel, Charmary Conquistador, UDT, Can. CDX, TD, show how to begin training for tracking. She has a short lead and the dog is working in very short grass with his nose to the scent.
Right: Annetta Cheek and her American Pit Bull Terrier, U-UD Cheek's Baroness, SchH III, showing winning tracking form.

Water Sports—Swimming and Boating

Like so many other activities, water sports with your dog can be as leisurely as taking a swim together or as vigorous as water games or even water rescue work, if you have a Newfoundland. Whatever you decide, most dogs can learn to love swimming if they are introduced to water gently.

Most dogs don't have to be taught to swim. Once they get into the water, they paddle naturally very much like babies and small children do when they get over their heads in water. However, most dogs need to be taught to swim alongside a person without clawing at the person and trying to climb onto the person's shoulders.

This is easily accomplished if you swim slowly alongside the dog so that your face and body present your profile to him. Don't thrash your arms wildly in the water. Do speak softly to him saying, "Easy, easy. That's a good boy." As long as you keep moving in a gentle forward direction and reassuring him that he's doing well, he'll quickly learn to maintain a slow steady pace without trying to climb onto you.

Make the beginning swims of short duration and never allow the dog to become excited when he's swimming with you. You can get excited once you reach shore again, but keep activities slow and gentle until the dog learns how to handle himself without becoming frantic or excited.

A Dalmatian enjoys a day of surf, sand and sun. Photo by Isabelle Francais.

Augie, an American Staffordshire Terrier owned by Daryl Davis, gets ready to dive into the family pool to fetch a Frisbee thrown by her owner's mother, Jane Keller. Photo by Daryl Davis.

Once the dog is confident of his ability to stay afloat for longer periods of time, you can lengthen the distance of each swim until you're swimming well together for several hundred yards.

Next you can introduce the dog to climbing out of the water onto a dock or into a boat. Begin this phase of training by letting him jump into and out of a rowboat on the beach. Next pull the rowboat down to the water's edge and let him experience the rocking of the boat as he clambers aboard.

Finally he'll be ready to learn how to use his front paws to pull himself into the boat when both he and

the boat are afloat. Initially you should be in the water also to help push him up into the boat as he tries to climb in. A few times of this and he'll be able to climb in all by himself with you in the boat urging him on.

Learning how to climb onto a dock from the water

This is Brush Breaking Beau, an English Springer Spaniel owned by Fred Grazioso, hitting the water. Photo by Isabelle Francais.

is done the same way except it's usually easier for the dog because, providing the dock is a stationary one, it won't rock when he climbs onto it.

Sharing your boating activities with your dog will progress naturally once he becomes an accomplished swimmer. First of all, having confidence in his ability in the water, the rocking of a boat won't unnerve him. There are, however, a few things he'll have to adjust to and you can help him with all of them.

For example, he must learn how to handle the footing of wet, slippery decks. Therefore, it would be wise to initiate his first few boat rides on calm days. Once he develops sea legs, he'll be as comfortable aboard your boat as you are.

Secondly, boaters must accept the fact that having a dog aboard means making arrangements for the dog's elimination habits. Very small dogs can be taught to use newspaper, but large dogs just can't handle urinating or def-

A gang of Labrador Retrievers splashing around in their local watering hole. Photo by Robert Smith.

ecating on-board. Thus they must be given the opportunity to go ashore several times a day.

I have a friend who has a boat and a big male Labrador Retriever named "Tar." My friend taught "Tar" to swim ashore, tend to his needs and return to the boat when he's finished. The command my friend uses for this whole process is, "Tar, do your thing!"

The dog loves his master and boating so much that he willingly obeys and hurries back to the boat as soon as he's finished. He never wanders around on the beach or annoys others: he thinks only of get-ting back to the boat so they can get underway again.

Actually, boating is one of the hobbies that is quite compatible with dog ownership. Since boats are privately owned, there are no "No dogs" rules. Dogs can be excluded, however, from public docks and beaches, but one can always find a place to give the dog some exercise in a quiet cove or along the shore of undeveloped beaches.

One final note about swimming for fun: as with humans, swimming is one of the best forms of exercise, particularly if the dog has some physical faults

Newfound-
lands are
alert swim-
mers and
instinctively
swim to the
rescue when
help is
needed.
Photo by
Robert
Pearcy.

such as hip dysplasia or weak shoulders. The weightlessness and slow rhythmic motion of paddling will build valuable muscle tissue without putting a strain on an already faulty structure.

One last reminder: dogs need to be bathed with clear water frequently as salt water dries their skin and can cause skin trouble later on.

For Newfoundland owners, there is water rescue work. In this, the dog swims out to rescue a "victim" who is drowning or has fallen overboard. In some cases, the dog carries a life ring to the person while in others the dog tows the person to shore while the "victim" holds onto the dog's tail.

Training water rescue dogs is complicated and lengthy. It should be done by experienced people only. For more information and details on other rescue dogs in your area, contact:

Mrs. George McDonnell
150 Sunset Ave.
Ridgewood, NJ 07450

Weight Pulling

Now here's a sport that's limited to the "he-men" of the dog population. Size isn't necessarily the criteria, however. There are some small breeds that are extremely strong and can pull amazingly heavy loads. Ability often depends on correct physical structure of the dog.

This activity is also one in which you should not become active until you have some experienced help. Making a dog pull a too-heavy load or a poorly balanced load can cause permanent, even crippling, injury to the dog.

There are records of St. Bernards and Malamutes pulling loads over 5000 pounds and a Bull Terrier that pulled a 2000-pound sled! But you can be sure these records were not made on a one-time basis. The dogs involved practiced regularly and the weight of their loads was increased gradually as the dogs' bodies developed muscle mass and strength.

Some sled-dog people have experience at weight pulling with their dogs and can help you find others in your own area who will guide you in getting started. They'll also tell you if they feel your dog is not a good candidate for the sport.

The only organization we know of in the United States that is devoted to weight pulling is the *International Weight Pulling Association*. You can write to them at PO Box 994, Greeley, CO 80632 for more information.

Liebenswert Amber, CD, TT, a weight-pulling Rottweiler, won Strongest Dog of All Breeds at the Houston KC in 1987 and Highest Percentage Pull at the 1987 American Rottweiler Club National Specialty. Owner, Liebenswert Rottweilers.

Yard Helpers

Dogs that help their owners outdoors can be invaluable in the amount of effort and man-hours they save their owners. They can be farm dogs that herd and/or protect flocks; they can pull carts laden with supplies and equipment; they can guard property and vehicles; they can help carry buckets and firewood. In fact, they can be willing helpers in many situations, providing the owner takes the time to teach the dog how to help and lets the dog know he's really appreciated.

If you'd like to involve your dog in helping you around the yard or farm, use the F.E.T.C.H. method to teach your dog to take, hold and carry objects.

Once your dog can do that, you can apply his carrying talents to your

Emma, a Standard Schnauzer owned by Marilee Schafer, helps with the gardening chores. Although the rake is bigger than Emma, she still manages to drag it over to her owner and therefore feels a part of the activities around the home. Photo by Marilee Schafer.

Having a large breed of dog around a suburban home really lightens the workload for owner Kimm Pontiff as Apollo hauls a heavy can out to the road. Photo by Charlotte Schwartz.

own needs. When taught motivationally, the dog will love carrying objects for you and you'll find him a valuable asset to your own activities around the place.

If pulling something is in the dog's future, you may want to try carting. Be sure he always pulls a balanced load, one that isn't too heavy for him, and that the cart is properly constructed for optimum performance by the dog.

Whatever you decide to teach your dog, use motivational methods, and praise lavishly when he performs any behavior that is close to your desired goal. He'll learn and perform quickly for you. (Using force methods in teaching any behav-

ior does not necessarily produce reliable workers.) Remember, the dog must want to perform a chore because he knows it pleases you and he likes doing it.

I know many dogs who help their owners around the yard and house and, in each case, the owner claims to have the smartest dog in the world! Actually, the dogs are smart because the owners took the time to teach their canine friends how to be helpful and, in building the dogs' self-confidence through achievements, the dogs are eager to participate in pack activities.

There's a big German Shepherd Dog named Thor

who carries filled trash bags to the curb twice a week for pickup. There's a tiny Toy Poodle named Pierre who picks up bits and pieces of trash on the lawn and deposits them into a wicker basket so the yard stays clean. Knight, a Labrador Retriever I know, carries firewood from the woodpile to the fireplace. Then, there's Spicey, a Miniature Schnauzer, who runs upstairs to the bedrooms or outside to the garage to beckon the family teenagers to come for dinner. And then there's Lacey, a Dachshund, who picks up her own toys at the end of each day and takes them to a basket in the family room where they belong.

These are only a sampling of the talented dogs I've had in obedience classes over the years. There are dozens more, which suggests that your own dog can be as talented and helpful as you help him to be. His talents will be limited only by your own imagination, so get busy. Let your friend be your helper!

If you have livestock and would like to involve your dog in work with the animals, you will be interested in the following:

National Stock Dog Maga zine
Rt. 1
Butler, IN 46721

New Skete's Rapscallion, UDT, Can. CD, TD, a German Shepherd owned by Lydia Strawbridge, carries firewood into the house. Photo by Judy Bard.

Your Dog's Growing Repertoire

Now that you've completed this book, decided on one or more activities for your dog, and possibly even taught him some of them, it's time to think about the future—yours and your dog's.

If you were to do nothing after teaching your dog one or more activities—and assuming he's enjoying his new lifestyle—you might notice several changes in his overall behavior and general attitude. The changes could occur suddenly or creep up so slowly that you don't notice them until they scream out at you.

What changes, you ask? The changes can manifest themselves in any one of a thousand ways. The dog seems restless or overly exuberant at times, sulks or fawns over you, exhibits mischievous behaviors that you haven't seen since he or she was a puppy or acts as though he were deeply hurt when you prepare to leave him and he knows it.

Let's explore the reason why first. Then we'll discuss some ways to prevent this from happening or correct it if it's already occurring. Either way, the poor pup is the one suffering the most and it's unnecessary.

You may recall reading initially in this book about the great need dogs have to develop a strong bond with their human pack. And, as I've explained, this bond is most easily built when dog and owner work together.

You may also remember that I referred to basic control and/or training as a key step in teaching a dog (or human) how to learn. Well, that's what has happened here. The dog has learned to learn, and now that he has, he's ready to

Sled dog team of Siberian Huskies owned by Tom Altievi. Photo by Isabelle Francais.

make learning a regular part of his life.

When that need isn't satisfied, he becomes frustrated and restless. And because he's learned to reason, he tries to figure out ways to get your attention. After all, he reasons, he received lots of attention while he was working with you, so if he does something to make you notice him perhaps you'll work with him again. Or even worse, just being devilish is getting him your attention when you notice his misdeeds and reprimand him. In either event, he's satisfying his basic need of interacting with you.

Don't be fooled into believing that dogs can think and reason to the same degree that man can reason, but you need to know that he is capable of doing some thinking on his own. And it becomes more apparent all the time that the extent of his reasoning ability is just enough to get him into trouble if you don't keep this in mind.

If you've noticed a change in your dog (or anticipate one), you can give yourself a pat on the back. You were a good teacher and you've created a willing, enthusiastic student. Now, let's talk about what can be done to

save your sanity and return the dog to his old self. And in the doing, we can help the dog develop even more of his latent talents.

The answer is to never stop teaching him new behaviors. For example, if you've chosen behaviors in the category of games and sports, allow him to participate in those activities on a regular basis. In addition, periodically introduce new ones.

For example, once he's learned to catch a ball, he can progress to catching other objects. If he's learned to carry a particular article for you, he can extend that behavior to carrying other things.

Ch. Bijan's Maximum Overdrive and Summerwind's Mint Condition, two Afghan Hounds owned by Sue Albert, practice gaiting. Photo by Isabelle Francais.

The dog that's doing helpful chores within the home or in the yard can spend a lifetime adding to his repertoire of jobs. If he carries an empty bucket for you, teach him the names of tools and let him fetch them for you when you need them. If carrying the trash bag to the backyard is his "thing," teach him to help tidy up the house as you do your daily cleaning.

The key to teaching any behavior is to break down the behavior into small parts. Then, one by one, patiently teach the dog each part. When he's mastered all the parts, put them together and he'll perform the behavior with confidence and ea-gerness.

Think of it this way: dogs are like humans—they want to be needed and need to be wanted.

For thousands of years, dogs have been living and working with mankind. And they've proved their worth and loyalty time and again. Now, your own dog is offering you the opportunity to enjoy one of the most unique experiences of a lifetime by becoming your devoted partner in whatever you choose to do.

I've said it before and I'll say it again—your dog's talents for working and playing with you are limited only by your own availability of time and imagination. Don't let your dog down, and don't sell yourself short: You and your pup can have the most successful and rewarding relationship you've ever had. All it takes is time, patience and the will to succeed.

Happy future!

THANKS

When writing a book such as this, one must rely on so many people to tell their stories, share their experiences and offer up their treasured photographs.

I want to thank the dozens of people who have done just that over the

A Miniature Poodle heeling on lead in the first level of obedience competition known as the Novice class. Photo by Judith Strom.

Terilyn's Just Another Cowboy, an Australian Shepherd owned by Kathy Hauer, having fun with a young playmate. Photo by Isabelle Francais.

years that I've been collecting material for this book. Since this is a book of ideas and instruction, it would not have become a reality without those folk.

In addition, I'd be remiss if I didn't mention my Editor, Andrew DePrisco, who recognized the goal I'd set for the book—to bring new ideas and motivation to the millions of dog owners who want more than just a walk in the park for their canine companions.

Andrew has helped me keep my thoughts on the final goal while attending to the hundreds of details that go into creating a book.

And finally I want to thank my family and friends who gave me help and support along the way, and to Ginger who kept me company all those long hours of writing and rewriting.

Thank you, all! You've helped make this book a reality.

Appendix: American Canine Sports Medicine Association

The American Canine Sports Medicine Association became a reality in 1991 when a group of veterinarians got together to exchange thoughts and ideas on the treatment and prevention of injuries to sporting and working dogs. In an interview with the association's President, Dr. Terry Terlep of Fort Myers, Florida, we gathered some fascinating information about the group.

As more dogs get involved in an ever-growing range of activities, the need for specialized veterinary care becomes greater. Just as with human sports medicine, dogs can and do suffer from a variety of injuries caused by those activities. Injuries to foot pads, hips, hocks, skin, noses and tails are just a few of them.

The ACSMA is dedicated to assembling the talents of veterinarians around the world who specialize in as many types of injuries as possible. Auburn University in Auburn, Alabama has an active, comprehensive research program for canine problems. The ACSMA works in conjunction with Auburn to treat and prevent these dog injuries.

Activities such as dog sledding, drug detection, swimming, hiking, jumping, arson detection, hunting and border patrol searching are just some of the areas involving dogs. And in many of these, dogs are susceptible to on-the-job injuries.

Membership in the organization consists of veterinarians, large corporations, interested lay persons and people actively involved in training and working with dogs. Members come from 27 countries and the number is increasing rapidly.

Anyone interested in more information or needing their assistance in locating a veterinary specialist can contact the Secretary, Dr. Ronald Stone, 12062 SW 117th Court, Suite 146, Miami, FL 33186. Telephone: 305-633-2402.

Index

Other Training Books from T.F.H. Publications, Inc.

TS-204
160 pages
Over 50 line drawings

TS-205
156 pages
130 full color photos

H-962
255 pages
23 full color photos,
64 black & white
photos

TW-113
256 pages
200 full color photos

SK-044
64 pages
50 full color photos

SK-025
96 pages
113 full color photos

TU-011
64 pages
50 full color photos

H-1016
224 pages
20 full color photos,
115 black & white
photos

All-Breed Books from T.F.H. Publications, Inc.

The T.F.H. all-breed dog books are the most comprehensive and colorful of all dog books available. The most famous of these recent publications, *The Atlas of Dog Breeds of the World*, written by Dr. Bonnie Wilcox and Chris Walkowicz, remains one of the most sought-after gift books and reference works in the dog world.

A very successful spinoff of the *Atlas*, the *Mini-Atlas of Dog Breeds* written by Andrew DePrisco and James B. Johnson, has been recommended by most national dog publications for its utility and reader-friendliness. It is the only accurate field guide for dog lovers.

Canine Lexicon by the authors of the *Mini-Atlas* is an up-to-date encyclopedic dictionary for the dog person. It is the most complete single volume on the dog ever published, covering more dog breeds than any other book as well as other relevant topics, including health, showing, training, breeding, anatomy, veterinary terms, and much more.

H-1106

TS-175

H-1091

TS-214
432 pages
Over 300 full color photos

TS-212
256 pages
Over 140 full color photos

TS-220
64 pages
50 full color photos

PS-607
254 pages
136 black & white photos,
10 line drawings

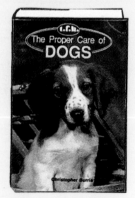

TW-102
256 pages
Over 200 full color photos

TS-130
160 pages
Over 50 full color photos

PS-872
240 pages
178 full color photos

H-1095
272 pages
160 full color photos

H-969
224 pages
105 black & white photos,
62 full color photos